I AM THE GUARDIAN OF THE FAITH

I AM THE GUARDIAN OF THE FAITH

Reported Apparitions of the Mother of God in Ecuador

Sister Isabel Bettwy

DECLARATION

The decree of the Congregation for the Propagation of the Faith, A.A.S. 58, 1186 (Approved by Pope Paul VI on October 14, 1966) states that the **Nihil Obstat** and **Imprimatur** are no longer required on publications that deal with private revelations, provided that they contain nothing contrary to faith and morals.

The author wishes to manifest her unconditional submission to the final authority and official judgment of the Magisterium of the Church, regarding the events presently under investigation in the Diocese of Cuenca, Ecuador, South America.

Cover Design: Art Mancuso

Published by:
Franciscan University Press
Steubenville, OH 43952
ISBN: 0-940535-46-7
UP-146

Printed in the United States of America

DEDICATION

''Give thanks to the Lord, for HE is good.
His love endures forever.''
Jeremiah 33:11

This book is dedicated to all those who have helped me in any way to complete this book, and who have encouraged and supported me along the way.

To mention individuals is risky and not really necessary. Their names are written in the book of heaven, for ''Blessed are the merciful, for theirs is the kingdom of heaven.''

TABLE OF CONTENTS

FOREWORD

I had the honor of being invited to Cuenca by the fervent group who are supporting the apparitions of Patricia Talbott, to assist them with the necessary discernment.

My visit in August, 1990, even though too short, and my study of the documents have made a very favorable impression on me. Patricia is sincere and quite transparent. She had not had any predisposition for the appearances. She has been constantly faithful and obedient in the daily difficulties of this much discussed event; she has been the source of controversy and she has been persecuted.

The fruit of the apparitions has revealed itself in several stages. A superficial and mundane Patricia gave up the group of models who found their glory in showing off their beauty. She gave priority to prayer and the poor, who are the focus of her life and her household.

Upset to the point of trying suicide as a revolt against her parents divorce, she found joy, faith and peace. Her parents today are reconciled and have been living together since September, 1990.

She herself, (Patricia) engaged during the apparitions, put off her marriage in order to accept a time of testing and retreat required, for discernment, by her spiritual director, Fr. Julio Teran, Rector of the Pontifical University. She has founded her family on Christ and the Church, in the light of Our Lady.

The fruits of conversion and involvement with service of the poor—a weekly, hot meal; a clothing dispensary; and help of all kinds—are remarkable in the Movement of the Guardian of the Faith.

The only thing I have not understood in Cuenca is how these apparitions, centered around the priority of the poor, in word and especially in deed, are able to be attacked under the title of the pastoral care of the poor. What ideology could cause this?

Sister Isabel Bettwy, Director of the Merciful Mother Association, tells us how she had been drawn to these apparitions, and she has carefully undertaken, with assistance and counsel, the writing of these apparitions.

I have appreciated the transparency, the spiritual penetration, and the brilliance of her account, which enables us to participate in the event from the inside. A second volume will contain documents, analysis and discernment of the problems posed by these apparitions.

Written in Medugorje, June 25, 1991
Tenth Anniversary of the Apparitions in Medugorje

R. Lauréntin

PREFACE

"I am the Guardian of the Faith." With these words the Holy Virgin Mary identified herself to Patricia Talbott, on August 28, 1988 in the city of Cuenca, Ecuador, in South America.

My involvement with the reported events in Ecuador began with the simple ring of a telephone. It was in early September 1989 that my friend Lourdes from Florida telephoned me on behalf of her friend Irene, a native of Ecuador, who had some questions about the reported apparitions of the Mother of God in her country. Would I go to Ecuador to look into the events there, and hopefully, answer her friend's questions?

I have been going to Medugorje, Jugoslavia, since October 1983 where six young people report that they began receiving visitations of the Mother of God in 1981. The tenth anniversary is approaching and four of them continue to receive daily visitations in the form of apparitions. During the many times I have been in Medugorje, I have had numerous opportunities to be present with the visionaries at the time of their reported apparitions. Because I have studied the events and edited several books about Medugorje and because of my frequent visits there, my Florida friend thought I would be able to answer her Ecuadorian friend's questions.

My first response was one of shock and dismay. "Please," I said, "I am not an expert on apparitions." But, I found myself asking, "What do you know about the events in Ecuador?"

"Very little, except that the blessings and the conversions are many. People are praying, returning to Church, and reconciling. The Spanish people are even praying with their servants," Lourdes responded. "I'll go. But not alone." I surprised myself with the quickness of my reply! In such important matters as discerning spiritual phenomena, I know that it is always prudent to involve more than one person. "Bring whomever you want. I am sure it will be all right," was her response.

The invitation was serious, and my response was immediate. I then began to pray to know who should accompany me. When I had a sense of a particular person, I told God that it wouldn't work, the person would never be able to get away and to please give me someone else's name. No other name was forthcoming and so, sometime later, I approached Fr. Michael Scanlan, T.O.R., the person whom I sensed should accompany me, and asked him if he would like to go to Ecuador. I told him the little I knew about the reported events there, and to my great surprise, he said, "When would we go?"

We determined that the best time would be for the First Saturday in February 1990, immediately after our Franciscan University Journey to the shrine of Our Lady of Guadalupe in Mexico City, Mexico. As the time drew near for us to leave for our Journey, Fr. Angelus Migliore, T.O.R. expressed a desire to go with us. The ease with which his arrangements were completed convinced me that our trip was going to be something special. We were not disappointed. And so, accompanied by Lourdes' husband, Raul, we made our first journey to Cuenca, Ecuador.

In March, I returned to Ecuador accompanied by Fr. Augustine Donegan, T.O.R., Lourdes and Raul. In April, I joined the visionary Patricia, her mother and some friends in Rome during which time Patricia gave Our Holy Father a personal message from the Blessed Mother. We then went on to Medugorje, Jugoslavia, for a personal visit. Upon our return to Rome, we went to Assisi for a brief visit. On all these occasions I was able to interview Patricia and the persons involved in the events surrounding the apparitions in Ecuador.

This book, the first of two, is a response to a personal call I experienced from the Holy Virgin to tell everyone about her visitations in Ecuador and, more importantly, to spread the messages which Our Mother is bringing through her countless apparitions in the world at this time in history. There is not as much detail in this book as one might hope for, since my purpose is to "get the word out" quickly. The second book will be more of a documentary, giving a chronology of the events, along with the messages, documents and reports, as they are available.

As in any translation, many times the other language version falls short of the meaning of the original. The messages in this book are translations from the Spanish and, while I have tried to be as accurate as possible to the original meaning, there are times where the translation seems wordy or even cumbersome.

Some people question the necessity of so many reported apparitions of the Mother of God in our day. I believe the answer is simple. It was at the foot of the Cross on Calvary that Jesus gave Mary to us as our Mother. St. John, in accepting her and taking her as his own, responded for each one of us. It was God the Father's plan that Mary, the Mother of Jesus, was to be our Mother also. And, as any good mother, she has the welfare of her children at heart. For this reason she comes to us, in our turmoil and in troubled times, with a Mother's call, a message of peace and a plea to return to her Son, Jesus Christ, who is our Lord and Savior.

Sister Isabel Bettwy

INTRODUCTION

The apparitions in Ecuador occurred over a brief eighteen month period, from August 1988 to March 1990, and did not become known widely in the United States until February, 1990. To help you read this book without losing the impact of the messages, I want to summarize for you the events and the messages. I have not attempted to quote all the messages in their entirety. That will be done in a later book. This book is intended to introduce you to the visionary, Patricia Talbott, or Pachi as her friends call her, to acquaint you with her experiences and to give you the messages Our Lady gave her for the world.

Summary

The apparitions of the Holy Virgin to Patricia Talbott began on August 24, 1988 and continued until March 3, 1990. At her last apparition on March 3, the Holy Virgin told Patricia that she would not see her again until her death, when Mary would come to take Patricia to heaven. Until that moment, Mary would speak to Patricia in her heart, but only at times of great need. On February 22, 1991, almost a full year since the last apparition, Patricia experienced her first locution. That particular day was an especially difficult one for Patricia. She was very depressed and she had even begun to doubt her faith. The Holy Virgin spoke to her, assuring her of her love, and then gave Patricia a message for all of us.

Patricia was just sixteen when the first apparition occurred. She was a high school student, and very active in a group of models. During the time of the apparitions, she continued to go to school, graduating in July of 1990, after the apparitions ended. Since then, she has married Andres Vega, her boy friend of many years. They live in Cuenca where Patricia is trying to fulfill the mission to the poor that the Holy Mother gave her. Her husband told me that he is prepared to support Patricia in this mission, and in fact, sees it as his mission also.

Location of the Apparitions

The apparitions began in Patricia's bedroom and continued there, as well as in various churches and chapels, until June of 1989, when they moved to a Garden spot in El Cajas, high up in the Andres Mountains. During the eighteen months of the apparitions, the Holy Virgin or Jesus appeared to and spoke to Patricia about one hundred times. More than two dozen apparitions have been recorded as occurring in Patricia's bedroom. Four apparitions took place in Mexico, eighteen occurred in chapels and churches in Cuenca, and a few others took place in chapels in Quito, Paute, and Guayaquil. After the location of the Garden in El Cajas, the majority of the apparitions happened there, with only several occurring elsewhere.

Frequency of the Apparitions

When Mary first began to appear to Patricia, there was no set schedule to her visits. Sometimes, the Holy Virgin would tell Patricia when and where she would visit her the next time, but, more often Patricia would sense an inner call from Our Lady summoning her to a particular place. Occasionally, this summons "interfered" with Patricia's schedule, at times, even calling her away from school. Once, Patricia told Jesus that she was very busy and He said, "Occupy yourself with My things, and I will occupy myself with your things."

During the last six months, after the apparitions began to occur at El Cajas the Holy Virgin came most frequently on Thursdays and Saturdays. These particular apparition times were known to the public and people would gather to be present when Our Lady would visit Patricia. Sometimes the people present would experience unusual phenomena. They report seeing bright lights in the sky, and the sun "dancing." On more than one occasion, people's hands and faces sparkled with a golden glow, as if from glitter, which could not be rubbed off.

On one occasion, thousands of persons saw the clouds form an image of the Blessed Mother. But, most importantly, the people responded to the grace that Mary was bringing them, and many began to change their lives.

The Messages

"Love God and love your neighbor as yourself," succinctly summarizes Our Lady's messages to Patricia. When I was in Cuenca, I obtained a little holy card that the followers of the apparition events had made to promulgate Mary's messages. The back of it reads:

> I am the Guardian of the Faith.
>
> Make your consecration to my Immaculate Heart and to the Merciful Heart of my Son.
>
> Put the Heart of Jesus in your homes.
>
> Pray the Rosary, which is a shield against evil. The Rosary is the most complete prayer, work to spread it.
>
> Use the scapular, which will protect you.
>
> Do penance and fast and with prayer, you will arrive at the Heart of my Son.
>
> Attend Mass and visit the Blessed Sacrament. The heart of my Son is very wounded.
>
> Offer your sufferings and penances to the Lord.
>
> Do not fear, the reign of God is near. Listen to the divine call.
>
> I ask you for peace, peace in your hearts. My children, you know my way, follow me. I will know how to illuminate your ways, my little souls.

In addition to this little summary, we can say that Mary's message carry with them warnings about coming chastisements and days of darkness, catastrophes, both natural and man-made, possible world war, and suffering in our Church and in the world. Our Holy Mother consistently reminds us that with prayer and fasting we can prevent wars and even natural catastrophes. "It all depends upon you," she says.

It is true that the messages Our Lady gave Patricia carry an urgency about them that should cause us to pause and to reflect on our personal life situation, where we are going, what we are doing, and with whom we are traveling on the road to eternal life. They should cause us to look at the world situation and make us realize that prayer and conversion are the only answers to the world's ills.

As I listened to Patricia summarize the messages and, as I have studied all of them, I realized two things. First, there was nothing new in them. Everything the Holy Mother said can be found in the Scriptures and the teachings of the Catholic Church. And second, the messages to Patricia seem to be more complete than any I have heard from other currently alleged apparitions. "It is all here," Fr. Michael, Fr. Angelus and I agreed as we listened to Patricia.

The Virgin's purpose is not to give us any new revelation—because there isn't any—but to spur us on to live the Gospel call to holiness, in a world that is tainted with evil, the result of original sin. I believe that the messages Mary gives in any particular place are for that place primarily and for the people she intends to hear them. Therefore, we should not compare the various messages, except for verification of basic truths. For example, why the Holy Virgin speaks about the scapular in one place and not in another is a question that is futile to try to answer, and takes our attention away from living the messages. Our focus should rather be upon living the messages in our daily life.

As any good mother, the Blessed Mother wants all her children to be happy here on this earth, and more importantly, to be happy with her when we reach the eternal kingdom. Therefore she cautions us against the pitfalls of life and gives us a means by which we can overcome the "world," the "flesh," and the "devil." She encourages us to "take up our cross" and to follow her Son, and at the same time, she reminds us that she is with us to help us carry the crosses in our lives. Just as she accompanied Jesus on the way to Calvary, so she is with us, as a Mother, along the way of our life, which will lead us ultimately to that moment when we pass from here to eternity, and we stand before the Divine Judge, who is Love itself.

The Holy Virgin's messages are messages of love. We see her love for each of us in them. Sometimes in Ecuador, she gave messages for certain individuals, whom she named. Other times, she spoke just to Patricia. But, the majority of the Virgin's messages to Patricia are for us, her children. And, that is how we should read them. We should hear our Mother speaking to us in each of the messages. Sometimes she is very specific, indicating her care about even the least detail in our lives. When she speaks about catastrophes and disasters, we should not fear. That is not her intention. Rather, she intends these messages to make us alert to the "signs of the times," and to bring us to deeper conversion now, and not to wait.

Furthermore, the messages from the Holy Mother should not be analyzed to the point that we waste energy trying to figure them out or trying to put together a time sequence of the events she speaks about. Our Mother says that everything depends upon us, and it is through our daily conversion that "it will be determined" when the hand of God acts in chastisement. You and I may never see "the great chastisement," for "we know not the day nor the hour." That is why the call is for NOW, and not for tomorrow.

As you read this book, see in it a message of love from our heavenly Mother, who loves us so much that she gave her only begotten Son so that we might have life, and have it abundantly. He, in turn, has given her to us. Listen carefully as she speaks to your heart. Now, to the beginning of our story.

CHAPTER ONE

THE BEGINNING

"Tell us your first experience of Mary's visits to you." The introductions were over and we settled down to the purpose of our visit. We listened intently as Patricia began to speak in a soft, gentle, meditative voice. There was a hint of a smile on her face, as she recalled for us those early days of her extraordinary visitations of the Virgin Mary.

Patricia Talbott awakened from a dream and saw her room filled with a bright light. She thought that she had not turned off the light before she went to sleep. But, she knew she had! The light was so strong that even when she covered her face with the blanket, the light shone through. She removed the blanket and peeked at the light again. She covered her face again and again, but the light continued to shine in her eyes.

Finally, she had the courage to look out from under the covers. The light was so bright, but within it she saw the figure of a beautiful lady. The beautiful lady said:

> Do not be afraid, I am your mother from heaven.Fold your hands across your chest and pray. Pray much for the peace of the world. I love you so much, my little child. Change. Pray for the priests and religious, because Satan is tempting them with sin, and confusion will be their principal challenge. Tomorrow at the first hour, I want you, my child, to make an altar in this place with blessed candles. I am the Guardian of the Faith and I will always be with you. Now, my little one, call your mother. Pray until dawn, as you have been taught. I love you so much, my little child.

Patricia said she became frightened, ''not like during a horror movie,'' but frightened. When the Lady told her to fold her hands across her chest and pray, Patricia began to pray rapidly, ''Our Father, who art in heaven...'' The Lady said, ''Not like that, like this,'' and started ''praying with me saying, very slowly, 'Our Father, who art in heaven...' ''

Ending her message, the beautiful lady departed, leaving behind the pleasing aroma of flowers which lasted for three days and could be sensed by everyone who came into the house.

Patricia did not understand the beautiful experience; she began to cry. She did as the beautiful lady asked and awakened her mother. After she related what had happened, they prayed until daylight. Both wondered if the beautiful lady would ever return. The mysterious visitation happened on Sunday, August 28, 1988, around 4:30 in the morning.

Later that same morning, Patricia, with several friends whom she had told about the experience, went to the Cathedral in the town center to buy candles for the little altar which she immediately arranged on top of the dresser in her bedroom.

Patricia shared the bedroom with her sister, Maria de Lourdes or Majita as her friends call her, who was at the family farm, Junguillia, and who knew nothing about Patricia's early morning experience until much later in the day when Patricia and her friend Paulina went there. Majita told me, ''I thought it was a dream, or an imagination of Patricia. I was scared to think about it. When I came back to Cuenca I asked my mother, and she told me the same thing.'' When Majita went to her room and saw the image of Our Lady of Fatima and the altar, she thought it was strange. She didn't like it that the entire dresser top had been made into an altar, because, ''I thought my sister wasn't normal, doing all these things. I thought it was a passing fancy of hers. I told her that she could have part of the top for the altar, and the rest was mine. She should not touch it.''

Patricia complied, moving the candles and images to one side. But, after a few days, Majita, who is ''neater and organized in my room and Patricia is not,'' had the feeling that she should rearrange the altar and make it pretty. And once again, the altar took up the whole dresser top!

Second Apparition

In the days that followed, the family began to pray together in front of the little altar which contained a crucifix, several different pictures of Our Lady and Jesus Christ, and some small stamps, or holy cards, along with candles and usually a fresh flower or two. On one of these occasions, Patricia was praying the Rosary with her mother, Majita and her little brother Sebastian when the Holy Virgin appeared to her again. Leaning backwards, with her face looking upwards and her hands extended, she had fallen into ecstasy. The beautiful Lady appeared but did not say anything to her.

This experience was the first time any of the family were with her during an apparition. Her posture was so strange that Sebastian became scared. Majita, too, felt frightened and didn't want to have anything to do with it. Sebastian began to cry. At that precise moment, Fernandito, Patricia's older brother, arrived home from a party. Hearing his little brother crying, he went upstairs to find them praying by candlelight. "Oh, Mommy, are you crazy? What are you trying to do? You are scaring my little brother." Fernandito wasn't at all interested in the visitations of the Mother of God to his sister.

Third Apparition

In early September, Patricia and her friend Chi Chi went to the town center to buy earrings and shoes in preparation for a trip to Costa Rica and Mexico. As they neared the Cathedral, Patricia said, "Let's go into the Cathedral. I feel that somebody is calling me." Kneeling down inside the Cathedral, Patricia saw the Holy Mother, in silhouette, not as a sharp image. Again, the Holy Mother did not speak, and after a few moments, she disappeared. Patricia did not understand what was happening or why she was having these unusual experiences.

CHAPTER TWO

PATRICIA TALBOTT

Patricia Talbott, third oldest child of Fernando Talbott and Carmen Borrero, wondered why the Holy Virgin Mary would choose to visit her. She wasn't particularly religious. In fact, she considered herself somewhat superficial in her practice of religion. She lived with her mother and two brothers and sister. Her parents had divorced several years earlier, and the divorce had been a cause of great anxiety and grief for the children.

Patricia didn't consider herself deserving a visitation from the Mother of God. Nor did she believe that such visitations took place in these days. In fact, one day at school, when her religion class was scheduled to see a video about the reported apparitions at Medugorje, Jugoslavia, Patricia heard what the tape was about and laughed. Instead of going to see the video, she left the school for home, saying, "That's ridiculous. Such things don't happen today." Some days later, her mother brought the same video home and wanted all her children to watch it. But, they each declined.

Fernandito and Maria de Lourdes, her older brother and sister, and Sebastian, her younger brother, didn't think Patricia was special. She was just their sister, whom they loved and who, now, was telling them she had not only seen the Holy Mother, but had talked with her! Fernandito was disturbed by such nonsense. Maria de Lourdes found it difficult to believe her sister's story. She knew her sister, and wondered what was happening to her. Little Sebastian, who had crawled into Majita's bed that first night, didn't fully understand what was happening, but he believed his sister from the beginning.

Sixteen years old, Patricia was an average young girl, preoccupied with thoughts of becoming a famous model and not particularly interested in school. According to her mother, Patricia always "had a big heart." She was a good girl, with many friends. She liked to dance and she liked to be with the young people. She liked "to be very pretty, all fixed up and wearing modern clothes all the time." If she went out three or four times a day, she would change her clothes each time. Before leaving the house, "she would stop in front of the mirror. If she didn't like how she looked, she would go upstairs and change."

In pursuit of her desire to be a model, Patricia had joined a group of young girls who modeled modern clothes designed after the typical, folkloric dress of the country. They were not the ordinary models as we would normally think of models. Rather, they represented their country at shows around the world, promoting tourism in such places as New York, Miami, Costa Rica, and Mexico. Patricia was excited about traveling and modeling. She is a beautiful young girl with a natural flair for being a model.

CHAPTER THREE

MEXICO CITY

In early October, the group of models were scheduled for shows in Costa Rica and Mexico City. Patricia's mother was concerned. These trips were costing more money than she had immediately available; and the girls were becoming more sophisticated than she wanted her sixteen-year-old daughter to be. They were becoming preoccupied with their appearance and less concerned about their school work. Her concerns were shared by other parents as well.

When the time came for Patricia to leave for the trip, she said to her mother, "Mommy, I don't know why, but I feel so afraid. I know I am going to need you so much."

It was so unlike her daughter. Normally, when Patricia left for a trip, she was light hearted and joking, and would say something like, "Goodbye, I am going. I am leaving this house where everybody drives me crazy. Goodbye." Carmencita, Patricia's mother, didn't know what to do. She couldn't go with her daughter. She had to find someone to look after her daughter. Among the young models was Bernardita Jerves who was in her late twenties. Carmencita caught sight of her, and even though she did not know her very well, she went to her and said, "Please Bernardita, take special care of my little girl. Something is happening to her. I don't know why, but she says she is afraid to be alone. Don't leave her, please. Stay with her and always take her by the hand." Bernardita assured Carmencita that she would look after Patricia. Through God's providence, Bernardita was to play an important role in the subsequent visitations to Patricia.

After the show in Costa Rica, the group moved on to Mexico City. In between shows, the girls became tourists and visited the popular places in and around the city. One of the first places they visited was the Cathedral in Zocalo Square. It was about 5:30 in the afternoon. The date was October 7, the Feast of Our Lady of the Rosary. Patricia and Bernardita stopped at the entrance of the Cathedral to buy a few little pictures of Our Lady of Guadalupe. Then, joining the group inside, they began to follow the guide through the Cathedral. At one point, Bernardita, who had been put in charge of the group that day, realized that one of the girls was missing. A quick look around revealed that it was Patricia. Worried, she began to look for her and soon she found her kneeling in front of the side altar of Our Lady of Guadalupe. "I felt funny because I didn't know that she was a girl who used to pray. So, when I saw her kneeling there, praying, I just left her on her own. I knew she would catch up with us."

A friend who was with Bernardita asked her if she knew what was happening with Patricia. Bernardita was shocked and surprised to learn that Patricia had been having visitations of the Virgin Mary. She felt strange. It just wasn't possible. After all, it was 1988. Apparitions couldn't happen in our day and age. And, even more frightening to her was the realization that the young girl she had agreed to look after was saying that she was seeing the Virgin.

As they were leaving the Cathedral, Bernardita ran to catch up with Patricia with the intention of asking her about what she had just heard. But when she reached Patricia she saw that she was crying. "Are you all right?" "I am all right. It happened to me again. Did you know?" Nodding her head and saying that she had just learned about it, Bernardita asked, "What is the Virgin saying?"

"It was in this apparition that I saw her for the first just like a real person, with a body, just like I see you now. Before, I heard her voice and saw her, as in a vision. But, today, she was a human person and she has such a beautiful voice. The Holy Virgin said, 'My little one, I am happy to see you. Don't be afraid.'"

In relating the experience to us, Patricia said that as she knelt to pray, with eyes closed, she experienced deep repentance for her sins, something she had never experienced before. She asked the Virgin why she had chosen her. Why had she not chosen someone who was intelligent, or someone who was holy? The Virgin told her the Jesus was a doctor, who came to save the sick. Patricia told us that at the time she felt sick in her soul, because she didn't know what it was like to live with Jesus. "At that moment, I had a vision. I saw many children of all the races of the world, naked. They had scars all over their little bodies. They were in a big field and there were fumes and smoke." Patricia was led to believe that is what we are like in God's eyes, little children, naked and wounded. He comes to save us and make us whole.

Our Lady tenderly held Patricia's hands in her own hands as she spoke to her. Mary told Patricia that she would not be able to touch her heavenly Mother again. "It will be a test of your faith. You will see and hear me just the same as now, but you will not be able to touch me," the Virgin said. Still holding Patricia's hands, the Holy Mother said:

> Pray much for the peace of the world, because it is now that it needs it more than ever. My little child, I am detaining the hand of my Son. Change and convert. I love you very much. Adios, my little daughter.

Bernardita and Patricia stayed up late that night talking and praying, not understanding what was really happening or why.

The next day, Saturday, October 8, the group visited the Shrine of Our Lady of Guadalupe. On the way to the new Basilica of Our Lady of Guadalupe, Patricia and Bernardita passed near a little shrine to Our Lady. Patricia sensed the Virgin calling her. Going to the shrine, she immediately fell to her knees because the Virgin was there, waiting for her. Other tourists looked at her strangely as they saw her fall to her knees. Her head was tilted back and her hands were extended with the palms facing upwards, as she looked up to the sky. Her body was rigid. She was obviously having an experience that took her out of touch with the world around her.

This time, Our Lady was real, and Patricia saw her just as she had in the Cathedral the day before. "What does she look like?" I asked. Patricia responded:

> She was barefooted and standing over a cloud. A blue veil covered her head and flowed down to her ankles. She wore a white skirt with a red blouse. Her eyes are big and long, the color of honey. Her hair, which comes out on both sides of the veil, is also honey colored. Her nose is small and straight and her lips are thin. Her face is fine and her skin is golden. She had a crown of twelve stars vertically around her head. Her arms were extended outwards and down, and she was holding the Rosary in her hands with the cross near her left hand. The Rosary is a brown color and the cross had a metal Christ.

Patricia told us that her description was the usual way the Holy Virgin appeared to her, but sometimes she had a crown of roses around her forehead and a rose on each foot. On special occasions, Patricia had seen the Virgin dressed completely in white.

Patricia wanted to reach out and touch the Lady, but she could not. Smiling, the Virgin said, "Thank you for having come, my little daughter." Then she gave Patricia a message and told her to give it to others.

> Pray the Rosary, which is a shield against evil. Use the scapular which will protect you. Place the Heart of Jesus in your homes for it will keep you united and in peace. Do penance and fast, and with prayer you will reach the heart of my Son. Go to Mass and visit the Blessed Sacrament. Pray to me and I will keep you under my mantle and in the Heart of my Son. I love you, my little daughter. Now go, for I await you inside.

Patricia obeyed and went inside the Basilica without noticing anyone or anything. She didn't even realize that Holy Mass was being celebrated. Catching up with the group who had been looking around the Basilica, Patricia and Bernardita went down the ramp to the moving walkway which passes in front of the beautiful tilma with the miraculous picture of Our Lady on it. She immediately fell to her knees, because the Holy

Virgin was there again. Bernardita, who had followed Patricia into the Church, tried to get her attention. However, Patricia was not aware of her presence, nor that of anyone else. She was quietly looking up, with her arms lifted slightly upwards, the palms of her hands opening upwards towards the sky. Again, it was obvious that she was seeing someone. Her friends who were near her had never seen her like this, and they were quite amazed.

The Virgin Mary expressed delight that Patricia had come, calling her again, ''My little soul.'' She said, ''In three days I will reveal to you the great secret in the Sanctuary on Tepeyac Hill. Put into practice my message. Go and give my message to them.'' The Virgin Mary told Patricia that she wanted her to tell everyone the message so they ''could have a conversion and convert themselves.''

Patricia wondered how she could be on Tepeyac Hill in three days because the group was scheduled to return to Ecuador that evening and she knew it was impossible for her to remain behind. She expressed her dilemma to the Holy Virgin who just smiled, and after blessing everyone in the Basilica, she departed.

That evening, the group went to the airport only to discover that the plane was overbooked, and all the girls had to remain in Mexico until the next flight, which wasn't for several days!

Patricia was beginning to experience change within herself. She usually would have spent any spare time on these trips shopping for new clothes. Instead, she returned to the shrine and, of course, went to Tepeyac Hill on the third day with three friends, including Bernardita. Most of the other girls went shopping.

Inside the church on Tepeyac, she knelt to pray. Shortly, the Holy Virgin appeared and said:

> My little daughter, you do not know how much it gladdens me that you are here. Now, daughter, now I will reveal to you my great secret which corresponds to the one revealed to the other visionaries. This secret you cannot write nor tell to anyone until I permit you.

Patricia listened intently as the Virgin told her the great secret. The Virgin then said:

> I put into your hands the great mission of the conversion and turn about of the world. I am now holding back the hand of my Son with the message that I have given you and if my children convert, the Heart of my Son will soften and the intensity can be diminished or be lost forever; if not, the great trial will come.

As Patricia pondered the message she had just been entrusted with, she felt something strange on her tongue. Putting her hand into her mouth to remove whatever it was, she was surprised to find in her hand a host. Shocked and thinking that she might be committing a sin by touching the Eucharist, she quickly put it back on her tongue. The Holy Virgin told Patricia that she had given her the Eucharist, and said:

> Now I leave you. Remember, that it is only a physical leave for I will always be with you and my Immaculate Heart will be united to yours enveloping it under my mantle. I love you much and I will never abandon you, my little daughter. Remember always that I will be the Guardian of the Faith.

Patricia knelt there, somewhat in shock, pondering the "secret" message she had been entrusted with. Her only consolation was the Eucharist she had just received, and the promise of the Holy Virgin that she would always be with her.

CHAPTER FOUR

THE DECISION

Patricia returned home to Cuenca believing that she would never see the beautiful lady again. She and Bernardita went to see the Archbishop of Cuenca to relate all that had been happening to her. His response was one of concern and great caution. Although he said he believed them, he was not able to make a judgment and asked them to be prudent. He was concerned that Patricia might be reacting to her parents' divorce and that she might be finding consolation in the "appearances of the Mother of God." He urged her to resume her normal life.

Wanting to be obedient, Patricia entered into her school life again, but she could not forget the beautiful and awesome experiences that she had had. She reflected on them and recounted them over and over again to family and friends. She also realized that she was beginning to lose the desire to be a model. Her preoccupation with herself and her looks lessened. She began to pray somewhat regularly now. After some time, Patricia came to the decision that she would no longer be a model. However, another show was approaching and she wondered how she could tell the person in charge that she was not going to be in it, and in fact, she wasn't going to be a model anymore. The experience of seeing the beautiful Lady from heaven and the knowledge of the great secret, coupled with a desire to put into practice the messages of the Virgin, had caused her to see her life in a different light.

On November 4, several days before the show, the woman in charge called to remind Patricia about it. Patricia was now faced with the dilemma of making known her decision. When she told the woman that she would not be taking part in the show, the person became upset and told her that she would call her back in one hour. At that time, she expected Patricia to have changed her mind, and she expected nothing less than an affirmative reply. Disturbed, Patricia went to her room to pray.

Kneeling before the images of Our Lady and Jesus, Patricia pleaded for help. The Holy Virgin appeared to her almost immediately. Patricia, who had resigned herself to the fact that she might never see the Holy Virgin again, thought it was her imagination. She reached out to touch the beautiful lady, but could not. She saw her as before, but she could not touch her. Then the Virgin said:

> I am your Mother from heaven, the Holy Virgin Mary, your Guardian of the Faith. You do not know how much it gladdens me to see you again, my little soul. I am here because of a need of yours. You have made a wise decision. Don't change your mind. Please don't continue in that.

The Virgin said that the world of modeling could not give Patricia what she should have for her life and that her decision was a good one. The Virgin continued:

> I am also here to reveal to you the date of the great chastisement which you can reveal to no one, to nobody. I love you very much. Now I leave you and remember that I will always be the Guardian of the Faith.

Patricia now knew that her decision was the right one, and therefore she could inform the director of her decision with certainty. But more importantly for her, she now believed that the visitations from the Mother of God were not over, and she could expect to see the Holy Virgin sometime again. She just didn't know when or where.

Meanwhile, some of the girls who had been in Mexico with Patricia began to share with their families and at school. They related how they saw Patricia that day in the Basilica, kneeling, looking up to the sky, and obviously conversing with someone. They shared their experience of hearing the message the Lady told Patricia to share with them, the message about praying the Rosary and fasting. As a result, a group of young people began to meet every Saturday to pray the Rosary. This was the beginning of the youth group that continues to meet weekly, even today, to share and to pray.

CHAPTER FIVE

THE DAYS THAT FOLLOWED

On December first, during a break in classes, Patricia visited the Blessed Sacrament in the chapel at the Dominican high school where she was a student. Going to the front of the Chapel, she knelt on the floor before the Blessed Sacrament and near the statue of Our Lady. She had hardly begun to pray when she felt a gentle breeze. Bowing her head humbly before the Lord, she wondered if the Holy Virgin would come. Almost immediately, the bright light appeared and the Virgin Mary came. Patricia's posture, once again, was unusual. Her head was thrown backwards as she looked up toward the ceiling.

There were a few students in the chapel who testify that they saw Patricia with her head tilted back, looking up and smiling. They also said that while she was in that posture, she began to write without looking at what she was writing. Patricia had never had the experience of writing while she was in ecstasy. After the apparition she had no recollection of writing, but when she looked at her notebook, the writing was clearly hers. Some may think this is unusual, but often visionaries, after an apparition, cannot recall all that they experienced or did while they were in the state of ecstasy.

The message read:

> My daughter, please listen to me very well. I want the Rosary to be prayed on December 8 in an open coliseum. See to it that this message is propagated everywhere, that it be done in your country and that you be the ones who carry in your heart the Rosary,

> which will be the imprint of God's love. Do not forget, in your city, have it done in an open space. Please, have all the schools be present there and pray the complete Rosary, the fifteen holy mysteries. I love you so much. Don't forget that I am the Guardian of the Faith. My little daughter, there always exists a happy tomorrow to a sad yesterday.

It was clear that this message was from the Holy Virgin, and that she wanted a public expression of love and devotion on December 8, the feast of the Immaculate Conception of the Blessed Virgin. But how was this message to be propagated to the entire city and other places in Ecuador? It was already the first of December.

Patricia and Bernardita, in whom Patricia had begun to confide, went to the Curia on the fifth of December to ask the authorization of the Bishop for the people and the schools to gather in an open place, to pray the Rosary as the Holy Virgin had requested. The Bishop would not authorize the event, based upon a reported supernatural experience and a subsequent request of the Holy Virgin. But, he said they were free to gather to pray, without the support of the Church. He even said that he would ask the priests and sisters of the city not to attend the event, as he did not want to sanction the reported apparitions in any way. Concerned about the people's response, he said that he wanted to protect Patricia, and himself. He told them they were free to gather but not to say that they were doing so because the request had come from heaven.

The word spread quickly, as people heard the reports of Patricia's apparitions and expressed interest in the events. Many gathered at the open area known as Templete, where the Holy Father had celebrated Mass during his visit to Ecuador in 1985. Making a little shrine with flowers around a statue of Our Lady of Fatima, they sang hymns to Our Lady and prayed the Rosary, at midday. Word of the request also spread throughout the country, and some people came from as far as Guayaquil, a coastal city four hours drive away. Persons who were there agree that about two thousand people had gathered, with only three day's notice, to pray the Rosary.

That size crowd attracted the media, and local reporters tried to discover which one of the girls was Patricia. But, people were praying fervently and most did not respond to their questions. Nobody really wanted to identify Patricia. But eventually someone did, and the press tried to talk with her. However, because the Bishop had asked Patricia and Bernardita not to get involved with the media, Patricia declined to be interviewed. She wanted to be obedient to her Bishop. Reports of the event, however, were carried by the local media, and the reported apparitions now became public knowledge.

The struggle to give up her old way of life was not easy for Patricia. She was fun loving and somewhat independent, and still was not very interested in school. She frequently went out with her friends instead of doing homework, and often would wonder why she should give up having so much fun, and doing the things that she had always wanted to do. But, the Holy Virgin kept appearing to her, and eventually, she said a wholehearted ''Yes'' to the Virgin and her requests. Her life began to change, as she tried to fulfill all that was being asked of her. She never lost her fun loving ways, and continued to go out with friends, but the emphasis was different now.

CHAPTER SIX

NEW DIMENSIONS

On December 15th, Patricia, her mother, Bernardita, and several women from Guayaquil were praying. In the middle of the second decade of the Rosary, they noticed that Patricia was in ecstasy. As they continued to pray, Patricia began to speak slowly and distinctly, but without her Cuencano accent:

> My Daughters, I love you very much. I am smiling while I am looking at how you pray, my daughters. Keep yourselves in my Immaculate Heart and the Merciful Heart of my Son. He is very sad to see that his message does not reach my little hearts. You are my chosen daughters. I love you very much, my daughters. My message has reached one of you more than the others. She has felt my presence more than the others. Put your rosaries on the front of my altar. They will be under my mantle, and blessed by my Heart and by the Heart of my Son. I ask you for peace; peace in your hearts, peace with each other and peace with your Father in heaven. You are my chosen daughters. You have in your hands the mission to transmit peace and the change of the world. Remember that I love you so much and that I am the Guardian of the Faith. Please stop being lukewarm. I want all to be strong in their faith. My little daughters, stop being selfish. Do not keep all that you have for yourselves. Give it and transmit it to the others. This is my message of peace.

Just as when Patricia did not remember writing the message in the school chapel, so now, she did not remember speaking aloud. This experience was another first for her, which she did not understand. We asked her if she had ever asked the Holy Virgin about these phenomena, the writing and speaking during the apparitions, and nodding her heard in a "No", she said it was not important to her. Rare as it may be, the obvious fact was that the Holy Mother was giving a message for her people, and she was using all means to do so. Patricia, even though she was of average intelligence, had never developed good study skills. I doubt that she would have been able to remember the messages, and the Holy Mother, knowing her limitations, chose other means to transmit her messages through Patricia, who had been chosen by God for this task.

Following the spoken message, one of the ladies immediately put her Rosary on the altar, and the others did the same. It was the first time Our Lady said she would bless rosaries. When the apparition was over, the group resumed the Rosary. The beautiful smell of flowers was present in the room.

Small groups of four and five persons began to gather to pray the Rosary. On the 24th of December, a friend and Patricia were praying at her house and the Virgin appeared to Patricia, and said:

> Guard my Heart. I am the Immaculate Heart of Mary. My children, it is near. Abandon yourselves and give yourselves to me. Everything is in your hands. My Son is waiting for you anxiously. Give yourselves to surrender. Love each other as He and I love you. Put your rosaries on the front of my altar. They are under my mantle. Have them always with you. The Rosary will be your shield; strive for its diffusion. I love you much, and remember that I am the Guardian of your Faith.

That was at midmorning. Later in the day, because it was the Vigil of Christmas, a larger group met to pray the Rosary at the Church of the Siervas de Maria (The Servants of Mary). Included among them were Bernardita, her sisters and mother, all of whom had left a family party to join in the prayers. Their leaving did not make their husbands happy. But the women had been touched by the messages of the Holy Virgin and had resolved to gather daily for the Rosary. Patricia was with them, of course. The presence of the Virgin was announced with the odor of sweet smelling incense and during the apparition, Patricia wrote:

> I am with you, my children. You do not know how happy the Heart of my Son becomes when your prayers rise. I am smiling because you are being sincere in your prayers. I love you very much, and remember that my Son Jesus is born in the depths of each heart. The Heavenly Father lives in Him, and do not close the door to the greatest happiness that humans can have. Thank you, thank you, children. I am the Guardian of your Faith.

The Holy Virgin frequently would address the situation or the persons who were present in such a way that they knew she was aware of what was going on. "I am smiling because you are being sincere in your prayers." Even a family Christmas party did not keep the women from gathering for prayer and Mary honored their sincerity with a smile.

At midmorning on Christmas Day, three friends came to Patricia's home to pray with her. Normally, Bernardita would have been there, but she could not join them because it was Christmas and she knew she should stay with her family. And so, she found time to be alone and to pray at home. During the fourth mystery of the Rosary, she heard a knock on the door of her house. Interrupting her prayer, she found a poor, little, old woman who asked for something to eat and for some clothes. Bernardita responded to her need with food and clothes, and in addition, gave her a scapular. She asked the lady to pray one Rosary a day. The poor, little, old woman responded, "If I could, it would be nice, but I don't know how to pray." Bernardita suggested that she speak with the priest in her town, San Miguel de Pilotas, and ask him to teach her. Returning to her room to resume the Rosary, Bernardita experienced the odor of flowers and candles even though she had not lit any candles that day, and there were no fresh flowers in the house.

Meanwhile, the group at Patricia's house were once again honored by the presence of Our Lady, who told Patricia:

> My Children, I ask you to continue praying just like today. I want you to pray together every day for at least

one hour. Today, the 25th of December, my Son has been born in a little portal that is your heart. Do not be afraid to accept the grace of my Son. I am with you. Today, try to go to a place where the Divine Word has not yet reached. In that way, you will make God, the Father, Son and Spirit, feel a bit of your love. Don't abandon Him. Rejoice in experiencing the love of God in your hearts. I love you and remember that I will always be the Guardian of your Faith.

The Rosary is the most complete prayer. Do not ask yourself why you pray it. Let it be your shield against the evil one who is at work. Do not detach yourselves of it. The Spirit of God descends upon you. Feel the warmth which enters your heart.

My warning comes to an end. I have already said so much. You have the great mission of the conversion of the world. Please, little children, make evil disappear. It is in your hands that the hand of my Son be detained or that you are going to suffer as strongly as the pain of His Heart. Do not be afraid, because I am with you. I will pour out the necessary graces on you. I love you much. Thank you, little children. My heart is filled with joy to see that four of my chosen ones are going to dispose themselves of everything to fulfill their mission.

Do not be afraid. Continue. God the Father, God the Son, and God the Holy Spirit will be in your words, in your actions whenever what you do is for God, in your work and in your studies. He will extend His hand to illumine your path. Do not desire more than what I give you. Receive what is mine with humility and with simple hearts.

Patricia immediately called Bernardita to tell her about the message and to ask her advice as to where they should go. Bernardita related the experience of the woman who had come to her door earlier that morning. For some unknown reason, Bernardita mentioned to Patricia that she was in the middle of the fourth mystery of the Rosary when the knock had come. Patricia realized that it was at the same point in the Rosary, the middle of the fourth decade, that the Virgin had appeared to her and had spoken to her. There seemed to be no question that the small group should take the Word of God to the little town, San Miguel de Pilotas, from which the poor lady had come. They went there immediately and found the people receptive to their message. They delighted in being able to teach the little children how to pray the Rosary, thus introducing them to the "Word of God."

Following this experience, the group of four agreed to pray together with Patricia every day, as Our Lady had requested. Bernardita was concerned because she had a family, and their needs had to be her first priority. She wondered how her husband would respond to her going every day to pray, especially when he was frequently at home at the agreed time. Deep in her heart, however, she knew that Our Lady would guide her in carrying out her decision. She was beginning to learn how to trust Mary for everything in her life.

The day after Christmas, when they were praying, the odor of incense and flowers permeated Patricia's house again. In a matter of minutes, the Holy Virgin appeared, and Patricia spoke this message; the beginning of which was for Bernardita:

> Bernardita, my daughter, do not be afraid. The Father knows the trial He gives humans and you must have the wisdom, faith, and patience to know how to endure all the divine obstacles. He is going to give you the hardest trials (in order for you) to reach His Divine Mercy, but that day you and your loved ones will be in the grace of the Beloved Kingdom.
>
> Children, continue praying. I want that in the place where you pray you organize the "wardrobe of the poor" and that you collect food for the poor. Children, do not abandon those who have nothing to eat or to wear, because in them is the kingdom of heaven. See in them your Father. Do not be afraid of judgment, because in you is your Father, Son and Spirit, and I will keep you under my mantle.
>
> My loved one, you are inside the Divine Salvation. Pray, pray and put into practice the Word. Help those who need it. Thus, from the just more will be asked

than from the unjust. I love you, and remember, I am the Guardian of the Faith. The Holy Spirit has poured out grace in your time. Remember, children, the day of Pentecost. I love you much. Do not fear, because the kingdom is near. Do not allow Satan to penetrate the heart which loves God.

Little children, know that all that you do benefits the world. Your prayers, penances, and fasts are impeding the third World War. Everything is as I have said before. It is in your hands. It depends on you whether the chastisement be as strong as the pain that my Son feels or that it be appeased with prayer.

Visit today all the churches and upon arriving at the last one, I will give one of you my sign. Love the Immaculate Heart of the Mother of Jesus. Do not permit evil. Do not be afraid. Feel the Divine Spirit in your little bodies. I love you very much and my Son is pleased with your prayers. I am the Guardian of the Faith.

This was the first message in which Our Lady mentioned war. ''It's in your (our) hands. It depends on you (us). . . Do not fear.'' Will we respond with prayer as the Virgin requests?

Obedient to the Virgin's wishes, the four started visiting churches, splitting up in two's, as it was already late in the afternoon and the churches would be closing soon. In the first church that Patricia and Bernardita went, that of the Siervas de Maria, Patricia wrote a message while they were praying:

Follow the example of being Servants of my Divine Heart and of the beloved heart of your Father. Upon arriving at the last one, one of my four beloved will receive a sign.

In the church of the Dominican nuns, Madre Catalinas de Roque, Patricia wrote two simple sentences.

My divine teaching is going to guide you to get to the one you have to find. Go now, continue.

The group had planned to meet at the last church, La Virgen de Bronce, at 6:15. They went into the little chapel and knelt down to pray the Our Father and Hail Mary. The Holy

Virgin appeared to Patricia as she had promised. Patricia first began to speak and then, in spite of the darkness of the chapel, she began to write the message. After Our Lady departed, Patricia handed the papers to Bernardita saying, "These are your messages." Bernardita remarked to us that it was an incredible experience. The messages were written in the dark, but they were written very straight.

Bernardita felt a bit faint, realizing that she was the one of whom the Virgin had spoken. At that time, she said that she did not understand why the Holy Mother had chosen her. The messages was:

> Bernardita, you know a part of the sacred chastisement. This is the sign. You, my beloved daughter, know already one of the ten sacred secrets. It is the dream, when in reality your spirit came out from your body and you saw all that can happen in that day. Do not talk about it until I ask you. My little soul, I grant you that one month before the thing happens you can notify all my children. But, this will happen only if you have a complete vision from your Father. If the contrary happens, you cannot reveal anything. I love you and only if the Father permits will you, one month before, tell the little souls from the entire world.

This message explained a dream Bernardita had near the end of November which she had not spoken about to anyone, except Patricia. She now understood that what she had seen was a part of the great chastisement. Never had anything so terrible or so horrible crossed through her mind as what she had seen happening in that dream. It was so real that when she woke up, her throat was dry and her hands were rigidly clenched in a fist over her heart. This dream, or nightmare to her, had disturbed her and she had spoken to Patricia about it, who cried, saying, "Oh, that is part of the chastisement." At the time, Bernardita didn't really understand what it all meant, and she dismissed it from her mind. But now, it became a little clearer to her.

The message also told Bernardita that she would be the one, not Patricia, who would reveal the coming of the chastisement, but only if she was given a vision from the Father. This vision would be her signal to tell everyone about the great chastisement which Patricia had been told about in Mexico, and which Bernardita had seen in her dreams, was near. At the time, she didn't understand why she would do it and not Patricia. But, since then, it has become clear to her, because one day Patricia told her, "The Holy Virgin said to me that I might be leaving before you." Patricia was speaking of her departure from this world, and Bernardita understood that. Bernardita now believed that Patricia would not be here to transmit the message.

The group continued to meet at various churches to pray the Rosary, being joined sometimes by other people. Frequently, the Holy Virgin would appear to Patricia. On December 27 in the chapel of the Carmelite Sisters at San Roque, she said:

> My daughters, please pay attention to the Divine Call. Don't fear. Today in a little way, you are fulfilling my wishes, but there is much to do to fulfill the Grace of the Father.
>
> Daughters, penetrate more deeply in prayer. Try to be discreet. Look for a Carmelite priest of advanced age, almost blind. He shall be your spiritual advisor. You have much need of priestly help. Pray very much for them because Satan is penetrating into the depths of the Holy Church.
>
> All these rosaries are under my mantle. Keep your rosaries on you because in this way you will not have temptation.
>
> I love you much, and do not abandon yourselves into the darkness. Feel the Spirit of the Father in the depths of your little souls. Do not permit the Kingdom of the Father to be blasphemed by the youth. Make them get away from drugs, alcohol, and music and fashions that insult the Divine Father.
>
> Daughters, you are my chosen ones. Do not be afraid, I am with you. Please, you must fulfill the mission.

The Holy Virgin then spoke a message for three young girls, asking them to detach themselves from vain things, and telling them to put themselves into the hands of the Father. She spoke private messages for several other people, reminding them that she was always with them as the Guardian of their faith.

CHAPTER SEVEN

THE MERCIFUL JESUS

Patricia never took the visits of Our Lady for granted. The experience of having Mary visit her was ever new, and something she looked forward to. On December 28, Patricia had a new experience, and one which brought her deep joy. Jesus himself appeared to her while she was praying with a woman from another city, and said:

> I would want you to make a song of joy out of your mission. I want you not to be saddened, but joyful because I am joyful. Do not fear, daughters.
>
> Be patient, tranquil. Do not run, because without thinking you get nothing; you may fall. Do not look after your good alone. Give yourselves over to my will. All that I say to you is because I look for something in you and everything is said. The time is short and there are no buts. It will be a hard and arduous mission but I will compensate you with my salvation.
>
> Know that He who speaks to you is your brother, Jesus Christ. Why do you sometimes doubt my presence? I have spoken to you many times, but my little souls, you are innocent in Divine Wisdom. Love my Mother because she holds back the fury of heaven. Love her in all the good that happens to you and be discreet.
>
> I am the Merciful Jesus, my heart is filled with mercy. Ask, children. I would like the day of my Mercy to be celebrated. Have in your homes an image of my Mer-

ciful Heart. Do not forget that the Father is good and that I came to the world for you, my beloved ones.

I am Jesus and know that all is in your hands. The time is short and I am already very wounded with all that my stray children have done. I love you, my chosen ones.

Patricia described Jesus as standing on a cloud, just as the Virgin does. His robe was white, and from his heart came forth two rays, one red and the other white. Like his mother, his skin was golden and his hair long and brown. His arms were extended outward and down, and Patricia saw in his hands and feet the wounds caused by the nails of crucifixion. His voice was smooth, sweet, and deep.

This first experience of Jesus was to be repeated several times in the next two years. But, just as with the Holy Virgin, the appearances of Jesus did not happen on a regular basis. Patricia was left to wonder when the next visitation would occur.

While listening to Patricia relate her experiences, I wondered if she had any sign, or how did she know, that the Holy Virgin or Jesus were going to appear to her, since there was no particular pattern to the visitations. She responded without hesitation that usually she saw a bright light, similar to what she experienced the first time in her bedroom. Sometimes, she felt the wind blowing, as she had experienced in Mexico. Periodically, Patricia said that she would experience a calling deep within herself, that she should go to a particular place or that she should stop what she was doing and go to pray. The Virgin would come at those times. Most often, the visitations would be during prayer, either at home or in a church. Patricia was never able to predict a visitation for certain. There was always an air of expectation in her, she said, and she longed for them to happen.

CHAPTER EIGHT

THE WORD SPREADS

As the events continued to unfold, word of the visitations circulated throughout the country of Ecuador in response to Our Lady's wishes:

> Propagate my message and do not fear being judged, nor that mockery hurt your heart, for there are few who can endure the obstacles and the trials of the Divine Father. Offer the Lord your sufferings and penances and remember that He too suffered for you. If you fall do not be afraid; rise again. Remember that Jesus fell three times before reaching Calvary.

Patricia and the group of young people, and people not so young, were being forewarned by the Holy Virgin that their task would not be easy. They would be misunderstood, ridiculed and even mocked. This happened. However, they were dauntless and continued changing their lives and trying to do everything Our Lady asked of them. She, in turn, often gave them the consolation of knowing that they were doing what she had asked and that their prayers brought her joy.

When the Holy Virgin gave Patricia messages for specific people, the messages always revealed that Mary knew the person's situation. Being a loving mother, she was concerned with all the events of their lives. For example:

> Bernardita, my daughter, do not be afraid. The Father knows the trial He gives humans and you must have wisdom, faith, and patience in order to endure the divine obstacles. He will give you the hardest trial to

reach His Divine Mercy, but that day you and your loved ones will be in the grace of the Beloved Kingdom.

Maria de Lourdes, you have your Mother's name. Why do you not try to be like her? You know that each prayer, each little work of yours pulls a thorn out of my Immaculate Heart. But with your selfishness you stab it twice.

My dear Sonja Maria, do you know how happy I feel when I see you so humble before my presence. You have the responsibility of accomplishing the mission with the youth.

The Holy Virgin often encouraged Patricia and the others to be examples by their lives, saying, "By the testimony of your life you will bring others to conversion." Our holy Mother knows the challenges we experience in trying to live the Gospel way of life, and she encourages us to be faithful to our call.

CHAPTER NINE

THE CRYING IMAGES AND THE OIL

On January 15, 1989 pictures and statues on Patricia's altar began to exude oil, and tears. Droplets of blood even formed on a crucifix. Majita, Patricia's sister, was the first to see the oil and told me, "I thought mommy or Pachi was putting the oil on the pictures."

Patricia had become quite ill with a high temperature and blisters in her mouth, and that day had gone to the clinic for an X-ray. Bernardita came by her house, and finding no one at home, went to Patricia's room to leave a rosebud for the Virgin, as she often did. She stayed only long enough to put the flower in a vase, and say a quick prayer and didn't notice that the pictures were exuding oil.

Meanwhile, before Majita left for the University, she had put some of her own holy cards on the altar—holy cards that she had since she was a little child. When she returned from college, she found all her stamps with oil, and the flower that Bernardita had put into the vase was open and oil was dropping from it. "It was so impressive, and Fernandito saw it also," Majita said.

Patricia and her mother returned; they called Bernardita, who came to see the pictures and her rose dropping oil. She immediately returned home and begged her husband to return with her to see the strange phenomenon. Up to that point, Bernardita's husband would have nothing to do with the reported apparitions, and thought his wife was a bit strange for being involved with Patricia. But, that day he came and saw for himself. Unable to explain it, his attitude toward the events and his wife's involvement began to change somewhat.

The next day, Patricia received a visitation from Our Lady who told her that the oil was an oil of salvation for those with strong faith, and the sick should be blessed with it.

That day, because of her illness Patricia was unable to attend a picnic at a friend's farm. Returning from the picnic, her friends found a line of cars, several blocks long, around Patricia's house. The word of the oil from the pictures had spread rapidly throughout the city, especially since images in several other people's homes had also begun to exude oil. People came from all over the city to see the unusual phenomenon. Not everyone believed it was miraculous.

Andres, Patricia's boyfriend who had recently returned from an extended stay in the United States, saw all the cars, and wondered what was going on. He was surprised to find people gathering in Patricia's outer yard, trying to get into her house. He saw that some persons were crying as they came away from her home. Knowing that Patricia was quite ill, he thought that she must have died. It was difficult for him to get through the crowd and when he finally managed to get to the gate, he found it locked. After pleading with the person who was inside the gate to let him in, and getting nowhere, he jumped the fence and once inside the courtyard was recognized by Patricia's family who took him inside to see Patricia. She told him about the miracle of the oil and tears on the pictures and the statues. Naturally, he was relieved to see that she was still alive, but he wondered about this new, strange phenomenon.

Andres had been out of the country when the apparitions began, and he wasn't sure he believed all that Patricia was telling him. He wanted to see the images and statues for himself. So, he went to Patricia's room where the altar was. His first thought when he saw the oil on the images was the Carmencita or Pachi or even Majita had put it there. Taking a picture that was dry from the altar, he returned to Patricia who was in her mother's bedroom. Patricia said, "Let's pray. The Holy Virgin is crying because of the lack of love in the world." They started to pray, but Andres did not take his attention off the dry picture of the Holy Shroud image of Christ he was holding in his hands. While they were praying, Andres saw oil coming out from the eyes, and, from around the crown of thorns, droplets of a liquid began to form. Up to that time, he had had his doubts about the apparitions. But, from that moment, he began to change his life, and he no longer doubted Patricia. He became one of her most loyal supporters.

On one of the days that Patricia was ill, a doctor came to the house to examine her. Seeing the phenomenon of the oil and the blood, he put some of each on cotton and took it to his laboratory to have it analyzed. His staff reported that they discovered red corpuscles in the blood, and human cells in the oil, but they could not identify the kind of oil.

Statues and pictures in several other homes in Cuenca began to exude oil and cry tears at the same time. The crying continued for some days, and on February 1, Our Lady told Patricia:

> The Father has allowed the grace of the holy oil, and my tears have been shed for the ingratitude of my little children due to the lack of unity, lack of love, and because each nation opens its doors to evil and to its own destruction. Love one another, children, and do not hurt the Father. I am the Guardian of the Faith.

On February 17, the Holy Virgin asked for a pilgrimage to all the houses where her statues exuded the oil, telling them that special graces were being given in those homes. ''Pray the fifteen decades of the Rosary. Take holy water with you and the image of Christ. A priest should be present.'' She also asked that they make a place to pray in their homes, an altar with a crucifix, her image, and that of St. Michael, the archangel. She said, ''You have a place to eat, a place to sleep, a place to cook, a place to receive your guests and so why not have a place to pray.'' They made the pilgrimage the next day, which was Sunday, just as the Holy Virgin had asked. Many people testify that they have received special graces in these homes.

The phenomenon of the pictures secreting oil and crying began again before the Holy Virgin's last appearance in March,

1990, and continued for several days. When Fr. Augustine and I arrived at Patricia's home in March, we sensed something unusual. Patricia's mother took us immediately to Patricia's room where the pictures were exuding oil. I had never seen the phenomenon before, even though I believe it happens, and has happened in other places that have been recognized by Church authorities. Before us, we saw droplets of a liquid forming in the eyes of the pictures and running down into cotton that was put into a dish below the pictures. It was awesome. I picked up several of the pictures and examined them carefully. I could find no visible cause for the oily tears. Fr. Augustine and I blessed each other with the oil, as the Virgin had said to do.

The next day, during the last apparition, the Virgin told Patricia that she was crying because many of her children were still so far away from God. She also said that just as she cried many years ago when she had to say goodbye to her Son, so now she was crying because she had to say goodbye to her children.

CHAPTER TEN

EL CAJAS

During one of the apparitions in Mexico, the Holy Virgin had asked Patricia to find a place where she could bless all her children and bring them the graces of conversion. Patricia had forgotten about the request until one day in February when the Holy Virgin reminded her about it. Shortly after, Bernardita and Patricia went to a nearby village, where they thought the place might be because a little Indian girl was reportedly seeing the Virgin also. However, they found a lot of commercialism there, and the Holy Virgin had said that the place should not be where "there was much commerce." And so, it wasn't until June 15, 1989 that Patricia, Bernardita and a few friends, some from Peru, began again to look for the place, for the sanctuary, as Our Lady called it. Patricia said, "I did not know what I was supposed to be looking for, so I prayed and asked God to lead us." They headed for Turi, one of the many beautiful mountains surrounding the city of Cuenca. As they neared the top of the Turi, they heard bells—loud bells coming from the northeast, the direction of a different mountain. There was nothing in the area that could be responsible for the ringing of bells. Even church bells weren't rung at that time of the day. Patricia, thinking the bells might be sign from the Holy Virgin, suggested they go in search of them.

As they drove up the other mountain, they observed a strange light in the sky, a light in the shape of an arrow, pointing to a place high up in the mountains. The light was so unusual that they thought it, like the bells, might be a sign, and they followed it until it appeared to point downward toward a huge rock in the middle of a large open area, part of a recreational region known as El Cajas.

The spot is high in the Andes Mountains, at an altitude of eleven thousand feet above sea level. The region is preserved from habitation, primarily because of the cold temperatures at that altitude. I was in awe when I saw it the first time on February 2, 1990. The beauty of creation speaks the beauty of the God who created it. Mountain ranges cross through each other creating a bowl-like area and, standing in the middle of it, praises of God for His beautiful creation welled up within me. It was cold, but sunny, and a bit windy. As I looked around, I realized I was completely surrounded by mountains. Cloud and mist moved between the mountain ranges, constantly changing the beautiful sky. The tops of mountains moved in and out of view as clouds passed over them. A geological team, whom I met there, pointed out one of the mountain ranges that is known locally as "the Madonna," because at a particular angle, the rock formations at the top of the mountain appear to form the Madonna kneeling in prayer. It was to this beautiful place that the bells and the light led Patricia and her friends that day.

Patricia and Bernardita were in separate cars. Part way up the mountain, Bernardita's car had trouble and never did reach El Cajas that day. But, as they waited for someone to come along to assist them, they saw a magnificent double rainbow in the sky. It was beautiful and brilliant and because they could see it from beginning to end, something most unusual, they ran through the fields to try to reach one end of it. Bernardita recalls that she looked at her watch and it was four-thirty in the afternoon.

Meanwhile, up at El Cajas, Patricia and the others headed for the rock. Patricia silently asked the Holy Virgin for a sign to know if this was the place for the sanctuary. Near the rock, Patricia said, "We will pray the Rosary, and if by the time we are finished we have no direction from Our Lady, we will return home, since I must study for tests. The Holy Virgin does not want me to make bad grades." She also realized that it was already late in the afternoon, four-thirty to be exact, and her mother would be looking for her. Carmen was not at home when Patricia and her friends had started on their search, and Patricia knew her mother would be concerned when she didn't find her at home.

Almost immediately as they began to pray, Patricia felt the wind on her face, and looking up, saw the Holy Virgin standing over the rock. Smiling, the Holy Virgin told Patricia that she had found the place where she would give her blessings to her children and lead souls to conversion saying:

> My daughter, you have sought me long enough and you have finally found me. In this holy place I will pour forth my blessings on all the pilgrims who come to me.
>
> Before this rock you must make an arch and under it you must place an image of myself which should measure one and two tenths meters in height. You will have many problems in this place, my daughter. Do not be preoccupied because the help that you are waiting for will come soon. As soon as possible, you must bring holy water and a priest to bless this place.
>
> I love you much, my dear children. You are the chosen of my heart and my little ones, the smallest among my children. Remember that I am your Mother from Heaven, the Holy Mary always Virgin, the Guardian of your Faith.

The Virgin asked that an area around the rock be fenced off and that "the Garden" be reserved as a holy place, a sanctuary. She said the garden would be a little piece of heaven, and only those she invited should come into it.

When Patricia returned home, her mother had just begun to wonder where she might be. She was happy to know that at last Patricia had found the place where they could all gather to receive the blessings of their heavenly mother and to receive the graces of conversion. Patricia said that, at that time, she began to realize that the events up to now were just the beginning, and much more was yet to come.

CHAPTER ELEVEN

THE FOLLOWERS

Bernardita

Bernardita Jerves de Ugalde was older than the rest of the group of models. She was the only one who was married, and she did not hesitate to leave her husband and two small children to travel with the group and participate in the fashion shows. This way of life appealed to her, and she was caught up in caring only for worldly things. She was cold spiritually. Her husband was secretly worried about her as he noticed her changing and becoming more preoccupied with modeling and traveling than she was with the family. But, he also noticed that when she returned from Mexico, she was different. Something had happened to her there.

Because Carmen Borrero, Patricia's mother, had asked Bernardita to take care of "my little girl" on the journey to Mexico, Bernardita was among the first persons to learn the details of the Holy Virgin's appearances to Patricia. When Patricia saw Our Lady at the outside shrine, it was Bernardita's arms that held her when the apparition was over. It was Bernardita who could feel Patricia's heart racing, as she held her tightly and let her cry. Bernardita was the first to hear the message Mary gave Patricia, with the mandate to "go and tell the others." Inside the Basilica, it was Bernardita who knelt down beside Patricia when she fell so forcibly to her knees upon seeing the Holy Virgin. Bernardita was the one who tried to move her, and found her to be rigid and not responding to her touch.

So, as they went inside the Basilica, Bernardita was experiencing something within herself, ''possibly fear, or possibly awe and wonder.'' She wasn't sure. She told us, ''I also had a sense that something was going to happen to me related to the Virgin. I was fearful because of the unknown, and fearful that I would have to accept the consequences of the things that surely would come after whatever it was that was happening.'' She sensed especially that there would be consequences for herself. Up until that time, her life had been easy and full of many things. She had everything. The more she had, the more she wanted, however. She was never satisfied with what she had. The list would grow and grow. Bernardita said:

> I knew that in that very moment that I was being asked to make a decision. A 'No' would have been very, very easy to say. But, luckily the 'No' didn't even flash into my mind. Instead, the 'Yes' welled up in me and the fear inside me suddenly left completely. I was in awe and wonder, and I humbly presented myself to the Holy Virgin. Looking up at Our Lady of Guadalupe, I saw a beautiful lady, as in the flesh. I said, ''Holy Virgin, if I am useful to you for whatever you want to do, please use me just like I am, and make of me whatever you want. If all that is happening to me is what I think, that you have come close to me through my friend, Patricia, so that I can help you, then I do want to help you. I want to do all that is your will. I don't feel that I am worthy of doing anything, but even knowing that, if you still want me, please take me for yourself. But I will never dare to say that I am worthy of all this.''

Finishing her prayer, Bernardita became aware of the people and the sounds around her. She saw Patricia get up with a big smile of satisfaction on her face, even though her eyes had ''a bit of a look of sadness.'' Instead of resuming the tour of the Basilica, Bernardita ran to buy as many holy cards of Our Lady of Guadalupe as she could before the place closed, thinking that she would leave one of them every place she went ''so that the Virgin would become known.'' When she looked at the image of the Holy Virgin on the cards, she realized that the image she had just seen when kneeling with Patricia was not exactly the same as was on the cards. The Virgin she had seen appeared to be alive and her head was tilted to the other side from what she saw on the pictures. She thought the picture was beautiful, but it looked like a dead image compared with what she had just seen. Even though the Virgin did not speak to her, she believed she had seen her "as a human person in the flesh," and from that moment on, Bernardita's life was different.

Carmen Borrero

Carmen Borrero, Patricia's mother, was a woman of prayer, a religious person. She had learned to turn more and more to the Lord for strength and guidance during the time of separation and divorce from her husband several years earlier.* She frequently sought out her spiritual director, the Bishop of Cuenca, Monsignor Luna, for guidance and advice. Carmen or Carmencita, did not force her spirituality on her children. She was content that they went to Sunday Mass and did the normal things required of any Catholic. Patricia had not captured her mother's piety.

However, when Carmen looked into her daughter's eyes that August morning when Patricia told her of the experience of the Virgin Mary, Carmen knew that Patricia was not lying. She knew her daughter. And so, without understanding what was going on, she joined her in prayer until dawn. The odor of roses that permeated the room also strengthened her belief that something had happened to her daughter during those early morning hours.

The trip to Mexico was a financial burden for Carmen and she had been able to gather only one hundred dollars for her daughter. When she gave the money to Patricia, she said, "Spend this wisely. Think every time you go to spend even one dollar, because this is all you have." And so, she was surprised at what she saw as she helped Patricia unpack her suitcase from the trip. There were no new clothes! It was most

*In September of 1990, Carmen Borrero and Fernando Talbott reunited in marriage and the family is once more complete.

unusual. Normally, Patricia would spend any money she had on new clothes for herself. This time, Carmen found a present for Sebastian, Patricia's little brother, some rosaries, holy cards and other small religious articles for her family and friends. Patricia's experience had to be real to have caused such a dramatic change in her daughter.

Shortly after her return from Mexico, Patricia told her mother about her decision to give up modeling. Carmen knew then that what was happening to Patricia was changing her, because modeling had been the most important thing in her life. Carmen became one of Patricia's strongest and most faithful supporters, never doubting her daughter's experiences.

The Young People

Word of Patricia's experience of the Holy Virgin spread quickly in Mexico to the other models. Some had seen her in the Basilica and went with her to Tepeyac. They began to believe, and started to pray. When the group returned to Cuenca, they all spoke about it, and word began to spread. As a result, young people began to gather to pray the Rosary at three o'clock on Saturdays at the Ramirez Center. The number varied from week to week, because for some of them, it was the thing to do on Saturday afternoons, and ''everyone was going.'' However, as time passed, the more serious ones continued to gather and to pray, while those who had come merely out of curiosity dropped away.

Parents began to wonder about their young sons and daughters. Were they really going to the Center to pray, or was something else going on? Were they secretly into drugs, or something like that? Some parents began to notice their children were changing. One mother said: ''My son used to slam the door in my face. We were not able to talk in a normal way. He would shout, always wanting the car and he would drive too fast. The music he played was so loud that it hurt my ears. Then he started going to the Rosary on Saturdays, because everyone else was going. Gradually, I noticed he was beginning to change. He became a lovable boy. Now, he is so nice to me.''

She, along with other parents, went to see for themselves what their sons and daughters were doing on Saturday afternoons. Bernardita related that one woman said, "I hope you don't mind that I am coming. I had to see what you do that has changed my son so much." While other parents related similar changes, some were disappointed as their young sons or daughters did not respond to the grace of conversion and eventually dropped out of the prayer group. The young people became known as "the Missionaries," a term derived from a message to Patricia while they were praying, in which the Holy Mother said, "I give you the mission of changing the world."

Young people continue to gather once or twice a week to pray the Rosary and to share their experiences of living the messages. There were about thirty persons at the meeting I attended in October, 1990. Another meeting had been held earlier in the day, because many of the young people are university students, and sometimes their classes conflict with the evening meeting. Some of the young people were not involved when the apparitions were actually taking place. The witness and the encouragement of other young people brought them to their first meeting, and they continue to come.

The group also meets to carry out their program of service to the poor and to those in prison, in response to a wish expressed by the Holy Virgin on December 26, 1988:

> I would like that in the place where you pray there be the wardrobe for the poor and that food be collected for the poor. Children, do not abandon those who have nothing to eat or to wear, because in them is the kingdom of heaven. See in them your Father. Do not be afraid of being judged because in you is the Father, the Son, and the Spirit and I will keep you under my mantle. . . .Pray, pray and put into practice the Word. Help those who need it.

When there is a need, the group gathers clothes for the "wardrobe." They began to serve meals to the poor on Saturdays as well. The number of poor coming to the meal has grown from just a handful to over one hundred, sometimes more and sometimes less. These young "missionaries" are learning how to "love God, and their neighbor as themselves," by living the Gospel, and serving those in need.

Gaston Ramirez Salcedo

When Bernardita returned from Mexico, she decided to tell each person in her family about her experience in Mexico, and about Patricia's experiences too. She didn't want some in her family to know about these events, and others not, and she didn't want anyone in her family to be able to say to her parents, "Why didn't you tell us about this?" She felt that the responsibility to tell them was hers and not her parents. One of the first persons she went to tell was her uncle, Gaston Ramirez Salcedo. Bernardita had grown close to her uncle during the previous year following the death of his elder son, her cousin Rafael, who had lost his life in a terrible accident. Rafael had been an exemplary young man, and his death had saddened everyone. Bernardita spent much time with her uncle, and so it was natural that he would be one of the first to hear her story. He was interested, and believed, from the beginning that the events might be real, and they were probably not the figment of the imagination of his niece or Patricia. When the young people needed a place to gather to pray on Saturday afternoons, Gaston offered the use of the Center which he had built several years earlier, as a type of Newman Center. It was available to the young people from the universities, and it was also used by the neighbors for sacramental celebrations, such as funerals and baptisms. It also houses Gaston's architectural offices.

Having listened intently to his niece, Gaston decided to capture Patricia's and Bernardita's experiences on video tape. He sensed the importance of the events without knowing why. He soon began to support the young people and Patricia in other ways than just allowing them to use the Center. He even risked his career as a politician when he "became involved" with the group since his actions were misinterpreted as being politically oriented and for personal gain.

As a member of the Social Christian Party, he had been Postmaster General of Ecuador from 1984 to 1986, and currently he was a city councilman. In 1987, because he believed there was a need to return to the constitution and its way of life, he had become more actively involved in the political life of the country.

Gaston is an architect and because of this, he had been consulted by a friend and local entrepreneur who was considering building a hotel along the mountain road being cut through from Cuenca to Guayaquil, a city on the coast. The road is the same one that leads to El Cajas, the site of the Garden where Our Lady appeared to Patricia. The entrepreneur had purchased the land and had begun planning the hotel months before the apparitions were reported as happening at El Cajas. The newspapers reported, however, that Gaston was supporting the events at Cajas so that he would gain personal wealth, joining in the building of a hotel for the "pilgrims" who would surely begin to come to the city. The location of the proposed hotel is not far from the Garden in El Cajas.

Gaston's involvement in the events surrounding the apparitions became important to him as he believed the messages were from the Mother of God. He experienced a deep conviction to live them out in his own life. In the beginning, his intention was just to help his niece and her friend Patricia. But, as time went by, he sensed a call to take a major role in promoting the events and distributing the messages. This involvement caused him to give up his political ambitions. When we were in Ecuador in February 1990, he had just announced that he would retire from politics. He did so in October of 1990. Gaston is one of the founders of the movement of "The Guardian of the Faith," a group that works to promulgate Our Lady's messages.

CHAPTER TWELVE

FIRST ANNIVERSARY AND AFTER

July 16, 1989

The sixteenth of July was a Sunday, and people from Quito and Ambata, along with Patricia, went to El Cajas at 10:00 in the morning. Patricia received a visit from Mary who gave a long message. There were some personal messages for individuals, and the Virgin requested a pilgrimage on the first anniversary of her appearances in Cuenca.

> I would like a procession to be made to this place on August the 28th because that day commemorates one year of my presence in this city with my little daughter. You must exchange hatred with peace, cowardliness with courage, and fear with love.

The Holy Virgin was accompanied by Michael and Gabriel, the Archangels whom she identified as her protectors. She asked prayers for the souls in purgatory and for the Holy Father, and for priests and religious, who she said should come into the Garden. Asking for penance, mortification, fasting and surrender to God's will, the Virgin invited all to come regularly on Saturdays and to bring others, too.

The Holy Virgin continued to visit Patricia saying that the pilgrims brought great joy to her heart. Her constant request was for prayer:

> The pilgrimage has brought much joy to my heart. Now more than ever they should pray. They should fast at least once a week. They should pray the Holy Rosary.

August 5, 1989

On August 5, Patricia and a large number of pilgrims gathered at El Cajas because that was the day Our Lady said was her birthday. The Holy Virgin came dressed completely in white. Patricia had brought her a birthday cake, and when she presented it to her she thought, "I hope you won't laugh, but we give people cakes on their birthdays." The Holy Virgin smiled and said:

> One day I was also human, my little one. The singing of my little ones is from their hearts. Their songs arrive to my soul. I am happy when you sing, my little ones.

August fifth was also one of the days on which Jesus appeared to Patricia and He commented on Mary's birthday saying that she is the most beautiful lady on earth and the most beautiful lady in heaven.

She is my mother. Love my Father more than anything else. Love my mother because she will take you to my heart. Tell all of them that I love them. Tell them all to convert faithfully, humbly, with simple hearts. I wait for you on the 28th on which it will be one year of the visit of my mother to your country. I want you to pray the Way of the Cross and the Rosary, by foot. Tell them all that I give them my love in their little hearts, that they will be messengers of my peace in the world, and that they should look for me out of love. The love of my mother will be my love for you.

When Patricia told the people that they were supposed to walk in pilgrimage to El Cajas on the anniversary, they told her that she must be wrong. However, she remained firm, and in a later message, Our Lady detailed the pilgrimage. It was to begin around 5:00 in the morning, with the people praying the Rosary, singing and praying the Way of the Cross.

During these days, Patricia had become quite ill again with blisters in her mouth, only this time they spread to the outside of her face. The pictures and a flower on her altar began to exude oil again. Patricia feared that the Virgin was crying because they hadn't done everything that she had requested.

Because the Holy Virgin had asked for a procession, Patricia thought she should inform the Archbishop about it. On the twenty-third of August, accompanied by Bernardita, she went to the Curia to speak with him. He informed them that he already knew what they were planning and that in the future they should not come to tell him what they were doing. They were free to do as they wished, but he wanted it known that their activities were totally apart from the Church. It saddened them because the Holy Virgin had told them they should stay close to the Church and to the Sacraments. Humbly, Patricia thanked him and then gave him a carnation which was dripping oil, explaining that it had come from her altar. He accepted it, but said nothing.

On Monday, the 28th of August, the first anniversary of Mary's apparition in Cuenca, more than six thousand persons, most of them from other cities and distant parts of Ecuador, gathered at the Garden sight. Many had walked from the spot on the mountain road indicated by Patricia as the place where they should begin the pilgrimage. They began at 5:00 in the morning as the Virgin had requested. The group included many young people, some of whom had been models with Patricia. They carried the statue of Our Lady on a flower-decked litter on their shoulders as they climbed the mountain. When they arrived at the entrance of the Garden, they dropped to their knees and walked into the Garden with the litter still on their shoulders. The crowd was pressing close and it was difficult for them to move.

That day, The Virgin called the little children, priests and religious and the young people to come into the Garden and she spoke a word of encouragement to each group. She spoke about her sorrow at the way the town of Cuenca had not received her:

> Today is the first anniversary of my presence in this holy city. My children you do not know the sorrow the inhabitants of this city cause me. You have not received with simple hearts the Love of my Son and my Love. My children, I will be with you for a very short time, due to the ingratitude of the people of Cuenca. I leave you with great sorrow in my heart. I will be on this hill for six months for my pilgrims. The

apparitions will be just once a month. My people of Cuenca have received me with great rejection. I ask you my children, those who have worked with me, to continue sharing that devotion with my little ones.

The Virgin told Patricia that she was the Sorrowful Mother who stood at the foot of the cross. Our sins nail Jesus' hands and feet to the cross, she said. As the Holy Virgin was saying this to Patricia, she actually saw Jesus on the cross and Mary at the foot of it.

Among her requests that day, Mary asked that on September 7 the people consecrate themselves to the Merciful Heart of her Son, Jesus, and to her Immaculate Heart, promising to pour out her love upon their little souls, "with little miracles for you, my sinners." Then she said she would come on the next six First Saturdays.

September 7, 1989

On the seventh of September, over one hundred thousand persons came for the pilgrimage. Word of the Virgin's request had been broadcast through the newspapers, radio and television, which had carried many reports of the pilgrimage and message of the 28th of August. Traffic was much greater than the police had expected and it was impossible for cars and buses to move up the mountain road. When the people realized that it was already 6:00 in the morning, they chose to leave their vehicles and walk—some twenty kilometers. It rained and the higher up the mountain they went, the colder it became. But, there were no reports of illness, even though many sick persons had made the journey on foot as well.

The Holy Virgin came, as she had promised, around 2:30 in the afternoon and spoke to Patricia, exhorting the people to peace. She asked that there be no sensationalism, fanaticism or mockery of her apparitions to Patricia. And, as usual, she requested prayer. There were many young people in the crowd and she asked them to be examples, to pray the Rosary and go to daily Mass. She reminded the sick of the Father's great love for them, and gave them her blessing. Assuring them that she expected them on the sixth of the next month, she departed with Michael and Gabriel, the Archangels who had accompanied her.

That day, many people reported seeing a strange phenomenon in the sky, the sun changed colors and moved rapidly toward them. This phenomenon happened several other times, and was observed by many people each time it happened.

The movement down the mountain was almost as difficult as the climb. People had little to eat or drink the entire day. Some young persons on motorcycles came by passing out chocolates and sandwiches. They had heard the announcements of the great traffic jam on the radio, and were putting into practice the Virgin's messages to do works of mercy.

September 9, 1989

Patricia and a small group of people went to El Cajas early on the morning of the ninth of September. Patricia felt called to do so. They found there a group of pure Indians from the region of Canyar. They had come by bus, leaving their village at 2:00 in the morning, just "to see the Virgin." Their plan was to return home walking because the bus had dropped them off, and continued on its way.

Patricia asked everyone to go into the Garden with her, and they prayed the Rosary. The Holy Virgin appeared to Patricia, smiling and telling them of her great love for them. "The way of salvation is hard, and there will be much suffering," she said. In this message, the Virgin spoke about the third world war which threatens the world, along with natural catastrophes and catastrophes created by man. She said they had to be strong, with faith like a rock.

The newspapers, radio and television had begun to report many disparaging things related to the apparitions. Even Church authorities spoke out against them. People who were involved with the apparitions were being made fun of. Just the opposite of what the Virgin had asked!

The Virgin said that many souls had been released from Purgatory through the procession, and the people should not allow the beautiful thing God had done among them to be ruined. She even expressed her own sorrow at what was taking place.

> Children, my heart is very wounded to see how they judge the apparitions. Little children, you must be humble, meek of heart. You should follow the Way, the Truth, and the Life, which is my Son Jesus. Get away from sin. Do not allow Satan to rob your hearts. Remember that I am the Guardian of your Faith.

October 7, 1989

On the seventh of October, the Feast of Our Lady of the Rosary, many people spent the night on the mountain. The Holy Virgin came to Patricia at 1:30 in the morning and gave her a long message in which she reminded everyone of her motherly love. Again, she spoke of the third world war which threatens the world, and of the great chastisements that are going to come on humanity. The Holy Virgin not only speaks of these kind of events, she also encourages prayer and repentance from sin, along with assuring us that she is protecting us under her mantle. Our faith is important, and she encourages us to spread peace. She also urges us to forgive others and to accept humiliations.

The next day, the eighth of October, was the anniversary of the day Bernardita saw Our Lady in the Basilica in Guadalupe. She and Patricia went privately to El Cajas late in the day. They found a group of youths who were bringing a small statue of Our Lady in pilgrimage to the Garden. As Patricia and Bernardita prayed in the Garden, the Holy Mother appeared to Patricia and asked them to repent from their hearts, and to replace hatred with peace. She also gave Patricia a message for Bernardita in which she asked her to forgive and to accept humiliations, and to pray for hardened hearts. Bernardita believes that the Virgin was referring to an experience she had had several days earlier which had hurt Bernardita and had caused her deep humiliation. She was encouraged and peaceful as they left the Garden that day.

November 4, 1989

Many people throughout Ecuador looked forward to the monthly visit of Our Lady and went to El Cajas for the pilgrimages. On November 4, the pilgrims waited throughout the night, not knowing when exactly the Holy Virgin would come. The night was especially cold. People commented that they did not feel the cold because they were deep in prayer.

At 5:00 in the morning, Patricia arrived. When she fell into ecstasy, a Capuchin priest who was present in the Garden, raised his hand in the form of a cross and said aloud, ''If you come in the name of God, bless us. If you do not come from God, leave in the name of Father, the Son and the Holy Spirit. Amen'' Immediately, Patricia began to speak in the now familiar, high pitched, sweet voice, saying:

> I bless you all my children, in the name of God the Father, in the name of God the Son and in the name of the Spirit of God.

It was the first time the Holy Virgin had begun a message with these words of blessing. Those present experienced the odor of roses.

The Holy Virgin continued, exhorting the people to prayer, saying that grave times were coming, and indeed, hard times were already taking place. She asked them to pray so that Satan would not reign in the world. Expressing her motherly love, and saying that she was the Guardian of their faith, she asked that they pray the Rosary three times each day, thus praying the complete Rosary everyday. The Virgin asked that they fast and share their love with those who do not have it. The messages contained nothing new. The Virgin's constant plea was for them to manifest their love of God in the way they loved others, and by doing so, Satan would not have reign over the world. She expressed the pain she experienced when she announces the coming of natural and man-made catastrophes.

CHAPTER THIRTEEN

SIGNS OF LOVE

On the eighth of November, Patricia was sitting on her bed trying to study. But, her thoughts turned to the Virgin Mary because she sensed Mary's presence. Momentarily, the Holy Mother appeared and told her to, "Get up and see in the little box under the feet of the little statue. There is my Sacred Son."

On Patricia's altar was a little statue of Our Lady of Fatima. It stood on a little wooden box. Rising, and going to the altar, Patricia picked up the little statue of Our Lady and opened the wooden box. There, she found a Sacred Host. Immediately, Patricia dropped to her knees and bowed her head in adoration. The Holy Virgin Mary told her that St. Michael, the Archangel, had put the Host in the box, and that she should pray before it everyday. Our Lady also told her not to show it to anyone without using great discretion.

Still in awe, Patricia called out to her family who came to see what she wanted. Carmencita, her mother, looked at the Host, and momentarily doubted because that kind of Host was not used in Ecuador anymore. Later that evening, Patricia spoke about the Sacred Host with a priest from Columbia who had been coming for the monthly pilgrimages. He told her to do what the Virgin had requested and to take it with her whenever she was leaving the city for any length of time.

So, the next week when Patricia went to Quito for surgery she took the Host with her, still in the little wooden box. When she showed it to her spiritual director, Fr. Julio Teran, Rector of the Pontifical University in Quito, he put the miraculous host in a golden pyx which he placed inside the wooden box and gave it back to Patricia.

While she was in Quito, Patricia and her mother were invited to visit with the Apostolic Nuncio. When Patricia showed the Host to the Nuncio, he looked quietly at it, and then said, "You should have the Host with you, and do everything the Holy Mother tells you to do." He, too, cautioned her to use much prudence, and not to show the Host to just anybody.

In February, 1990, when we were with Patricia, she showed the Sacred Host to Fr. Michael, Fr. Angelus and me, and told us how it was left miraculously on her altar by St. Michael, the Archangel. She asked us not to talk about the Host with anyone, telling us what the Holy Mother had said about it. Patricia followed the Holy Mother's request and the Nuncio's advice and until the time we visited Patricia in February, she had not shown the Host to anyone. Sometimes, her mother would ask Patricia if she wanted to show the Host to some special visitor, but Patricia would always decline.

Patricia did not know what was to happen to the Host, until sometime later, Jesus told her, "In the last month it (the Host) should be consumed by the inhabitants of this house, and a priest should distribute it."

On March 4, 1990, the day after the last apparition of Mary, Fr. Teran celebrated a private Mass in the family home, during which the Host was consumed by Patricia, her mother, her brothers and sister, Bernardita, and another close family friend. Each person was able to receive just a tiny portion of the Host, but for each, the experience was very deep, beyond their ability to express it adequately in words.

December 1989

On the first Saturday of December, 1989, there was another large procession, with six thousand persons gathering at El Cajas. The night and day were spent in prayer. At 7:00 in the evening, the Holy Virgin appeared to Patricia in the Garden, and reminding the people that she is their mother from heaven, the Guardian of their faith, saying, "I am the start of love, peace, and humility. I am very happy with all that you do for me." She asked them to learn to forgive one another and to remove resentment from their hearts. "Days of darkness are near, but greater than the darkness of the earth is the darkness of the soul," she said.

> Why, because you do not keep lit the lamp of the heart with the light of my son Jesus. You must learn how to make amends for your faults. When you fall, you must not remain sitting, but you must get up. The greatest fault is when you realize that you have fallen and you don't get up.

During the time of apparition, the Blessed Virgin gave her blessing three times, once at the beginning of the message, another in the middle of the message, and another as she ended and said, "Goodbye."

On that day, a phenomena occurred that was witnessed by thousands of persons. The clouds parted and a great light formed the image of Our Lady of the Miraculous Medal in the sky. Some persons who were on the mountain testify that this experience of seeing Our Lady in the sky was the beginning of their belief in what Patricia was saying. Up to this point, they had come merely out of curiosity.

On December 8, the Feast of the Immaculate Conception of Mary, more than fifteen thousand people gathered on the mountain. Even though it was not a First Saturday, there was an expectancy that perhaps the Holy Mother would visit Patricia, because the day was a special feast of Our Lady. At eight o'clock in the evening, the Holy Mother did appear to Patricia and asked everyone to remove all stain of sin from their souls. She exhorted them again to accept suffering because it draws us closer to God. She asked them to pray the Rosary, to go to daily Mass, to forgive one another, to unite their families in prayer, and to help those in need. She then said that she would wait for them on the twelfth of the month. After giving a personal message for one of the priests, the Holy Virgin departed giving everyone her blessing.

On the twelfth of December, Feast of Our Lady of Guadalupe, people, among them people from Mexico, gathered at El Cajas to wait for the Holy Mother to appear to Patricia. At eight o'clock in the evening, Patricia entered the Garden and began to pray. Mary appeared and gave Patricia a beautiful message.

> My little children, I love you very much and I ask you to extend your hands to God as when a little child, learning to walk, extends his arms to his mother. Little children, let yourselves be enveloped with the love of God. Fly with the wings of the Lord, gallop in the beautiful field of God.

Patricia said that as the Virgin was saying this, she had a vision of a beautiful, green field with white horses galloping across it.

The Holy Virgin asked the people to remove curiosity and sensationalism from their hearts and to replace them with love. ''Be meek, simple and humble,'' she said.

Her message was that of a mother who loves her children, and who wants only what is best for them.

> Little children, I am your Mother from heaven, your Guardian of the faith. Learn the humility of my son, Juan Diego, the smallest of my children who is with me in eternity. Children, why do you take so long to change? Do not leave for tomorrow what you can do today. Begin today with firm steps towards a faithful conversion, a conversion of love. . . .don't cover the soul with a mask of hatred, resentment, pride. Remove the cancer of pride because it is killing your souls.

Blessing everyone, the Holy Virgin asked them to come on the twenty-fourth of December. Then she departed.

On December twenty-fourth, about one thousand people gathered in vigil in the Garden. The Holy Virgin appeared to Patricia and said:

> Today is your night of Peace. . . Little children, how you have waited for this moment. What I give you is the peace of the heart. Know how to accept it. What I give you is to know how to forgive, and to accept the forgiveness of others. What I give you is the beginning of Wisdom. Accept it.

After giving a private message for one of the priests, the Holy Virgin said that she wanted all the pilgrims to come into the Garden. Their sinfulness should not stop them from coming. She asked that they come to her feet and the feet of her Son Jesus in an orderly manner, two by two, asking for their needs. Patricia related this to the people, who quietly lined up and waited their turn to go into the Garden. Some people stayed through the night and into the next day, Christmas, assisting people in and out of the Garden.

Patricia went as often as she could to the Garden in El Cajas. Sometimes, the Holy Mother would appear to her, and other times she would not. Occasionally, during the apparitions, Patricia would have visions, often seeing what Our lady was speaking about. On one occasion, Patricia saw the Holy Family at their home in Nazareth. When Jesus sat down at the dinner table with Mary and Joseph, Jesus looked at Joseph with love and admiration in his eyes. She heard Jesus pray before they began to eat, saying:

> I thank you, Father for the food we are about to take. I thank father Joseph who has obtained this food with his work. Bless, Father, the hands which have prepared this food. Give food to those who don't have it, and hunger for you to those who do. Amen.

CHAPTER FOURTEEN

THE LAST THREE MONTHS

January 1990

January 6, 1990, feast of the Epiphany, first Saturday of the New Year, more than ten thousand pilgrims spent the night at El Cajas, many of whom had walked the last five miles in pilgrimage, as the Holy Virgin had requested. The Holy Virgin came to Patricia at 4:00 in the morning as she knelt in the Garden in prayer. The message spoke of hard times, chastisements, the Mercy of God, and so much more:

> My little children, little of heart, today you bring your offering to my Son Jesus as the Magi did, the offering of your souls, souls that will be renewed in peace, love and forgiveness. Little children, learn how to look, to see with the eyes of God. Learn to feel God's embrace. Learn how to see the smile of God.
>
> . . .Children, there is much sorrow in my heart, for many natural catastrophes and others created by man are coming. Hard times are already taking place, a short decade filled with suffering. Children, the third world war is near. Do not frighten your hearts, because the peace of God is with you. . . .Forgive all men. Understand the mercy of God. Understand my petitions. All that I have told you is because God the Father has asked me to. Children, the time is short, very short. Conversion must be faithful. Remove all evil sentiments because Satan penetrates in them. Remove them with the Presence of God in your souls. Children, give

> thanks to God for what you have. . . . In these last days in which I will be present, because my leave is near, you must fill your hearts with the light of my Son, so that a desolation of faith will not exist. . . . Children, my Son Jesus imposes his hands on your heads to take away hatred, pride, bitterness. Accept it. . . . Goodbye my little ones. I bless you in the name of God the Father in the name of God the Son, and of the Spirit of God. Goodbye, little ones.

During the month of January, some of the pictures on Patricia's altar sweat tears again, and the crucifix bled. Patricia discovered a drop of blood on the Sacred Host on her altar.

February 1990

In February, following Mass for the Feast of the Presentation of Jesus in the Temple, thousands of pilgrims began to drive to El Cajas on Friday evening, since the Holy Virgin had requested a vigil in preparation for her visit to Patricia. There was some confusion, and many people thought this month was the last time Our Lady would appear to Patricia. Pilgrims came from many cities all over Equador, as well as from a few foreign countries. Traffic became a major problem, and cars were not able to move up the mountain. As in September, the people began to walk to the Garden site, this time a distance of ten miles, praying and singing, and carrying the litters bearing statues of the Sacred Heart of Jesus and Our Lady on their shoulders.

After a very cold, rainy night, many people thought the Virgin would come early on Saturday. However, she waited until three-twenty in the afternoon before summoning Patricia to the Garden. Her message was spoken, as in previous months:

> Little children, do not be anguished. Sew happiness and give joy to the world. My little children, I love you much. I am happy with what you have offered on this day. Jesus is present here and in each one of your hearts that has been purified today. We have begun

the hard times. It will be ten very sad years. Time is short.

I am expecting you the first Saturday of March and my physical presence among you will conclude then. But I will always stay here to pour out my blessings upon you. Atheism and materialism are eating the world. My priests, religious, laity, work in the work of my Son, Jesus and convert souls. . . . In the hands of priests and religious is the salvation of souls. Evangelize with the light of my Son, Jesus. Have pity on my Son in order that my Son will have pity on you before the Father.

Giving a blessing in the name of the Trinity, the Holy Virgin departed. Patricia told us that during February, the last month before Mary's final visit, she would not receive any apparitions of Our Lady. The Holy Virgin was preparing her for the day when her visits would cease.

Unexpected Events

During the month of February, Archbishop Luna reopened and enlarged the Diocesan Commission to study the events being reported by Patricia and by many others, who had experienced graces of conversion, healings, and the return to the Sacraments. Some members of the Commission were present in El Cajas, and in the Garden during the February and March pilgrimages and apparitions.

A statue of Our Lady, Guardian of the Faith, which had been made according to Patricia's description of the way she sees Our Lady, began to cry and continued doing so for three days. Photographs of the statue taken during these days present a very life-like image of Our Lady. On March second many of the pictures on Patricia's altar began to exude oil, and cry again.

During this month, while Our Lady did not appear to Patricia, her Son, Jesus did. This was totally unexpected, but his visits brought joy amidst her sorrow as the first Saturday of March approached.

One morning, Patricia and a friend were assisting at daily Mass at the Church of La Merced. One of the side altars depicts the scourging of Jesus at the pillar the night before his crucifixion. During the Mass, Patricia glanced at the scene and Jesus came alive and began to speak to her saying:

> My little one, when you believe that I love you the least, that is in when I love you the most. I carry you in my arms as a little girl. I am in all human beings, in all of you.

Then, coming down from the scene, Jesus led Patricia in spirit to the front of the Cathedral in Cuenca, outside of which there are many beggars asking for money. Pointing out one in particular, Jesus said that many times, at the end of a day, that beggar had collected barely enough for one piece of bread. Often, He said, the beggars are hungry and cold. Jesus told her:

> I am in each of them. I feel hungry, cold and thirsty. I need warmth. Feel me as your brother, as your friend, as your Father. . .

Jesus then brought Patricia back to the Church of the Merced where she realized that people were going to receive Holy Communion. When she approached the priest to receive, she recognized him as one of the poor persons she had seen at the Cathedral. However, as she looked at his eyes, she saw only Jesus. Patricia knew that she was being called to pray, in a special way, for the poor, and for priests who, while embodying Jesus Christ, are also ''beggars.''

From almost the beginning of the apparitions, the Holy Mother would speak periodically to Patricia about her mission to the poor and the beggars. In April 1990, during a visit to Rome, Patricia told me she wanted to visit Assisi because, ''St. Francis had the same mission I have to the poor, the beggars and the lepers.''

Early in the morning on February 8, Patricia went to El Cajas to pray. Our Lord appeared to her and said, ''Occupy yourself with My things, and I will occupy myself with your things.'' Jesus told her that we must learn to carry our cross with love, just as He had carried his with love. In this way we would be able to hope for redemption. He also told her that one of the signs that would point to the nearness of the chastisements would be a comet which would pass by the earth. He said that His mother was preparing us for His coming.

On the Feast of Our Lady of Lourdes, February 11, Patricia went to the Garden early in the evening. Many other people were there also, because it was a feast day of Our Lady. Our Lord appeared to Patricia, bringing with Him an aroma of incense. Patricia told the people, ''Our Lord is happy with what we are doing to honor His mother on her day. He asks us to come with much humility of heart. He pours out His blessings on all present and He asks that you enter the Garden with devotion.'' The people looked forward to the times when they would be invited into the Garden, because Mary had said, ''It is like a little piece of heaven,'' but only those she invited could go into it.

March 1990

For the March 3, 1990 apparition, over one hundred fifteen thousand pilgrims went to El Cajas. Some had even gone there several days before and pitched tents in anticipation of spending the night in vigil. It was an extremely cold and rainy night. At twelve noon, Patricia came into the Garden, walking on her knees as was her custom. Once, I asked her why she did so, and she just looked at me and smiled and said, ''She asked me to.''

Professional television cameras had never been permitted in the Garden before. Prior to this, only one home-type video camera recorded the monthly apparitions. Priests and sisters were permitted in the Garden as usual. There was an air of expectancy both inside and outside the Garden.

Earlier in the day, the statues of the Sacred Heart of Jesus and Mary had been brought in procession through the crowd by priests who carried the flower-decked litters on their shoulders. When they arrived at the gate of the Garden, the priests fell to their knees, with the litters still on their shoulders, and slowly moved up the muddy path in the Garden. The people greeted Jesus and Mary by waving white handkerchiefs as the procession moved through the crowd. It was a beautiful testimony of their love for Jesus and Mary, and a magnificent sight to behold.

Patricia and those with her had been advised to wear identical clothes so that as they moved through the crowd on the way to the Garden, it would be difficult to recognize Patricia. Someone had threatened to kill her. But, once inside the Garden, Patricia removed her head scarf as she began to pray.

Immediately, she went into ecstasy, with her body arched back and her face looking up to the sky. She began to speak the message:

> My little children, small of heart, today I have brought you here so that you may love the Heart of my Son, Jesus. Little children, I love you very much. Today is the day of my physical departure, but my spiritual retreat will never be. I will be with you always, little children. I ask for prayer, fasting, penance. Help those in most need. Children, in the end God will triumph over all things. Remember the first commandment of my Son, Jesus: Love one another, and love God above all things. Little children, I ask for peace, pardon, and conversion.
>
> Children, priests and religious, help in the conversion of the world, the redemption of souls, the purification. Children, the laity, help in the conversions. Young people, be examples of light.
>
> Carry the Cross in your hearts. Put on humility. Children, white doves of peace, be the light.
>
> The sick are indeed chosen by God, chosen for the redemption of the world.
>
> Little children, I love you so much that even for me it gives me sorrow to say goodbye to you. Children, I am not going to leave you ever, because I will be here and I will wait for you always, as each month, as each time that you have come here to leave your sadnesses, your sorrows, and your anguishes.
>
> Little children, each representative of each country, I ask you to take with you the message of peace, love and understanding.

Patricia, the model.

Interviewing Patricia.
Irene Davalos, Patricia and Fr. Angelus.

Patricia; Fernandito, Patricia's brother; Sr. Isabel Bettwy; Fr. Michael Scanlan, T.O.R.; and Fr. Angelus Migliore, T.O.R.

Fr. Angelus, Fr. Michael, Gaston Ramirez Salcedo.

The garden area at El Cajas.

Priests and Sisters praying in the Garden
before the apparition of Mary on February 3, 1990.

El Cajas during early morning hours on February 3, 1990.

El Cajas during the early afternoon on February 3, 1990.

Celebrating the sacrament of Penance.

Bernardita and Patricia inside the Garden during the apparition on February 3, 1990.

Patricia with Fr. Augustine Donegan, T.O.R.

Priests carrying the litters
with the statues of Jesus and Mary into the Garden.
Inside the Garden area, they walked on their knees.

Panoramic view of El Cajas midmorning on March 3, 1990.

Inside the Garden, just before the apparition.

Patricia in ecstasy.

Patricia singing the *Ave Maria* to Our Lady.

On Mt. Podbrdo (Apparition Mountain) in Medugorje. Two friends, Patricia and her mother, Carmencita.

Patricia, Fr. Petar, O.F.M., Carmencita (Patricia's mother) in Medugorje, Yugoslavia.

Medugorje - Two visionaries: Marija and Patricia.

Medugorje - Two visionaries: Patricia and Ivan.

Patricia holding the painting which she gave to Our Holy Father, Pope John Paul II. The artist, Jose Murillo, depicted Mary the way Patricia usually saw her.

The group from Ecuador with Msgr. Thu before the general audience in March 1990.

Patricia kissing the hand of Pope John Paul II. Bernardita is on her right and Carmencita is on her left.

Patricia presenting the personal message from Our Lady.

At the moment when the Holy Father said to Patricia:
"We are together."

Fr. Julio Teran, S.J.,
blessing a family prior to their leaving El Cajas.

Pilgrims leaving El Cajas,
after the First Saturday pilgrimage on November 3, 1990.

Bernardita and her daughter, Maria de Lourdes, praying during the morning of November 3, 1990.

Fr. Pancho, Bernardita, Fr. Rene Laurentin, Patricia and Fr. Julio Dutari Teran, S.J., in the Garden in late July, 1990.

The Youth Group who meet to pray,
share and reflect on the meaning of Mary's messages.

The Saturday meal for the mendigos (poor).

At the family farm, Junguillia. Andres, Patricia, Fernandito, Patricia's father, Fernando; Carmencita, Patricia's mother; Maria de Lourdes (Majita), and Sebastian in the center front.

Andres, Sr. Isabel and Patricia at Junguillia.

Gaston Ramirez Salcedo, Carmencita, and Anita, Gaston's wife, with Patricia and Andres.

Patricia and Andres
at a Dominican retreat house,
where Patricia had an apparition of Mary.

Patricia, before her marriage
in front of the altar in her bedroom.

Patricia and Andres cutting the wedding cake.

Children, I give you the blessing of the all-powerful God, Father, Son and Holy Spirit. Come always to visit me. Never abandon me little ones because I love you so much, so much.

At the end of all the apparitions in the world, I will leave a great sign in this place and in all those where I have been. Goodbye my little ones. Goodbye my children.

Because of the television cameras and the radio microphones, the message was broadcast over the entire area as it was being given by Our Lady. People began to weep when they heard Our Lady express her sorrow at having to leave physically. The message ended, and there was a brief period when Patricia remained in obvious ecstasy. Then, she began to sing the *Ave Maria*. Some people joined her, not realizing that the apparition was still taking place. When Patricia finished singing, the apparition ended for Patricia and Mary was no longer visible to her. However, Patricia continued to hear Our Lady's voice, as in a locution. After a period of time, Patricia turned to the priests and told them the Holy Mother requested that they give their priestly blessing to all the faithful. Only after they did so did Patricia stand to leave the Garden. There was much weeping as Patricia, her family and a few friends who had accompanied her departed. The message was played over and over again for people to hear. Television and radio broadcasts repeated it for several days throughout the country.

During the time when Patricia was hearing Our Lady but was not seeing her, the Holy Virgin gave her the description and the dimensions of the sanctuary she wanted to be built at El Cajas, a sanctuary "in which the Father, Son and Holy Spirit will be adored." The Holy Virgin also told Patricia that it would take much time before this would come to be, and there would be many difficulties before it could happen.

The Holy Mother also told Patricia that she would be in the Garden on Thursdays and Saturdays as always, but especially at the hours of the Angelus. Patricia told us later, "She awaits us the first Saturday of each month, and wants a pilgrimage beginning at five o'clock in the morning. Just as we have been doing. There will be no messages, but she will give us her blessing at the Angelus time. Her physical presence has ended, but her spirit and motherly love will be with us."

During this time of hearing Mary's voice, Patricia was able to carry on a conversation with Her. She asked Our Lady why she was crying again, referring to the statue and the pictures on her altar. Our Lady responded:

> My tears are poured out for the evil that exists in the world, through atheism and materialism, through adoring false gods, through ignoring the Word of God and the Sacraments.
>
> I have not come in order that they recognize me without recognizing my Son Jesus in their heart. I am the Mother of all who believe and who do not believe in me.
>
> The pain from having told you what is coming to the world fills my heart with sadness. I also was a Mother and I felt the pain of saying goodbye to my Son. In the same way, today, I feel the pain of saying goodbye to you, because I am your mother.

The Holy Virgin also said that with the apparitions now over, we, like the apostles after the Ascension of Christ, should go out evangelizing the world with the Word of God in one hand and her messages in the other.

At one point during the apparition, Patricia bent over, almost prostrating herself. Afterwards, she told us that she was so overwhelmed with the beauty of the apparition that she bowed in adoration before the heavenly scene. She described it in the following way:

> Jesus was at the top. Below Him was the Holy Virgin, surrounded by seven angels. They were dressed all in white. There was a brilliant halo behind Jesus and Mary. The scene was beautiful and resplendent. At her feet and to her left was a little man, poorly clothed with a brown tunic that had a belt around it. He had a beard and he was very thin. You could see he was very poor, and he was holding a skull in one hand and a Rosary in the other hand. I didn't know who he was, but I

said 'hello.' The Holy Virgin told me it was St. Francis of Assisi.

Patricia told us that the Virgin said her contact with Patricia would be much deeper and she would feel the Virgin much closer than before. Patricia asked, ''Virgin Mother, I will never see you again?'' And Our Lady said, ''No. Only on the day of your death.''

Patricia continued: ''I will not see her physically until the day of my death when she will come to pick me up and take me to heaven. She said that she would speak to me in my heart when strictly necessary, but that I would be with her, in the happiest moments and in the saddest moments.

She told me that I knew already what I was supposed to do. She expects that I will never go far from her, that I will never let go of her hand, because she will always be holding mine.''

CHAPTER FIFTEEN

RELATIONS WITH CHURCH AUTHORITIES

In January 1989 when the pictures and statues began to secrete the oil, the events did not escape the press. It was at this time that Archbishop Luna appointed a Diocesan Commission of three priests to investigate the reported events, and also to investigate the reports of a nine year old peasant girl in another part of the Diocese who also was claiming visitations from the Holy Virgin.

Patricia and her mother were called to testify before the Commission in late February. Bernardita was sent for on March 6, 1989, along with Paulina, the first friend Patricia had confided in about the apparitions that Sunday morning in August and who went with her to buy candles at the Cathedral. Bernardita offered the Commission her journal which she had begun to keep while they were in Mexico, and in which she had made almost daily entries. Even though she was told that she would be sent for at another time, that did not happen, and the Commission did not request to read her journal.

Patricia and her mother were called to the Diocesan Offices on April 18, 1989, where Archbishop Luna and two members of the Commission gave them their conclusions. While they recognized her sincerity, the Commission was not able to say that the manifestations of the Holy Virgin were supernatural, nor were the messages from heaven. On April 20, the report was published in the newspapers. Naturally, the report was painful for Patricia, her family, Bernardita and all those who had become involved with the apparitions and who had experienced great personal graces. Nevertheless, Patricia and

Bernardita humbly accepted the report, knowing that they should be obedient to the Church. "It (obedience to Church authorities) is what the Holy Virgin asks of us," they said.

In February, 1990, after the pilgrimages of the previous six months which brought thousands of pilgrims from Ecuador and other countries to El Cajas, the Bishop reopened the Diocesan investigation of the reported apparitions to Patricia. At that time, he also enlarged the number of persons on the commission to include five priests and three doctors.

When I was in Ecuador in October 1990, I had an opportunity to meet with the five priest members of the commission. An internationally known and recognized linguist had done an analysis of Patricia's voice when she spoke the message during the apparitions. The voice, as has been noted earlier in this book, is different from her own. It is higher pitched and more delicate, "sweet" to the ears, as it has been described by many. The linguist had sent me his analysis and I was able to present it to the Commission. They received it and then asked me many questions. Several of them had seen me in the Garden in March when they were present for the last apparition to Patricia. I assured them of our prayers, because their work and conclusions would have an effect not only on the people of Ecuador, but on the whole world.

Episcopal Conference of Ecuador

On two occasions, the Episcopal Conference of Ecuador, made up of all the Bishops of the country, has issued statements encouraging the faithful to maintain the unity of the Faith in the midst of differing opinions concerning the authenticity of the apparitions. They encouraged true Marian devotion and spirituality in keeping with the teachings of the Catholic Church. Persons are free to follow the messages and the reported requests of Our Lady in so far as they are not in conflict with existing Church practices. The position of the Church in these matters is always to "wait and see" and to test the effect of the reported apparitions on the faith life of the followers. "By their fruits you shall know them," is the Scriptural guideline for judging such events. The ultimate authority for making a judgment rests with the Bishop of the Diocese, and our stance must be submission to it.

The Carmelite Priest

In response to our question about a spiritual director, Patricia related that on December 27, 1988, while she was praying with a small group of people at the Chapel of the Madres Catalinas in San Roque, Our Lady had requested that she "look for a Carmelite priest of advanced age, almost blind. He shall be your spiritual advisor. You need priestly help. Pray much for them because Satan is penetrating into the depths of the Holy Church."

Patricia and Bernardita did not know any Carmelite priests. They were not aware that the Archbishop was a Carmelite. However, one day as a result of a dream in which she saw an "old priest, almost blind," in a brown habit, Bernardita asked a priest who was wearing the same habit, what order he belonged to. He told her that he was a Carmelite. She described the "old priest, almost blind" to him and he told her that there was a Carmelite priest in Quito who fit her description. His name was Fr. Lorenzo, and he was from Spain. Bernardita called her Aunt in Quito and described the priest, asking her if she could locate him for them. Her Aunt immediately recognized the priest as being Fr. Lorenzo, telling Bernardita that he rarely sees people and that he is difficult to get along with.

Hearing that an old, almost blind priest really existed, Patricia and Bernardita decided to go to Quito to look for Fr. Lorenzo. They went to the Carmelite church, and when an old priest opened the door, they were surprised to learn that he was Fr. Lorenzo. They told him of the request of the Virgin, and of Bernardita's dream. He was not easy to talk with. But, he listened and then looked at them and said, "You mean the Holy Virgin chose me for something?" They responded that it seemed that way. He folded his hands and started to pray, thanking the Virgin. Then, his manner with them changed completely and he became very gentle, saying that he would help them. They told him all about the apparitions and Mary's messages. Bernardita promised to send him everything she had written down, which she did.

Sometime later, she received a letter from Fr. Lorenzo in which he asked them not to communicate with him again. They could not understand the change in his attitude.

In late April, Patricia was in Quito and she was able to see Fr. Lorenzo briefly. He explained that his superiors would not permit him to have any communication with them. His mail was being censored, and they were threatening to send him back to Spain if he communicated with them in any way. All these events were confusing to Patricia and to Bernardita. They did not understand the Virgin's request and their inability to carry it out.

When we returned to Cuenca in March, 1990, we were surprised to learn of the sudden death of Fr. Lorenzo. In the meantime, the Virgin had told Patricia that Fr. Julio Teran, a Jesuit who is the Rector of the Pontifical University in Quito, would be her spiritual director.

Vow of Silence

In September 1989, at the suggestion of a priest, a member of the Bishop's Commission, and encouraged by Gaston Ramirez, Patricia signed a "vow of silence" promising Archbishop Luna not to speak publicly about the apparitions. It was believed a vow of silence was necessary because of the adverse publicity and newspaper articles that were attacking everyone involved in the events surrounding the reported apparitions. Factions were forming and nobody believed it was healthy for either Patricia or the Church in Cuenca. Patricia asked all those who were supporting her to agree to the silence also. Bernardita told us, "I had the idea that in signing this document, the Holy Virgin did not let Patricia on her own. When I read the part 'I abandon myself to God the Father, to Jesus and to Mary,' I thought we didn't have anything to fear, because we are in their hands. Patricia's agreeing to make the vow of silence is also a great proof of her obedience to the Church, as our Mother Mary has asked us. She will continue guiding us." Now that the apparitions are over, Patricia still honors the vow of silence.

CHAPTER SIXTEEN

THE MESSAGES

Our Lady's first message to Patricia was a request to pray for peace. The Virgin said, "It is now that the world needs it (peace) most." Prayer and peace seem to be Mary's universal request in all the current, reported apparitions. The apparition messages in Ecuador are no exception.

The majority of Our Lady's messages to Patricia were intended for everyone. In Guadalupe, the Holy Virgin said to Patricia, "Go now and give them this message." Sometimes, Our Lady would say things like, "Tell them. . ." or "My loved ones. . ." or "I ask all my children. . ." Phrases such as these indicate that the Virgin's messages to Patricia were intended for more than Patricia. The fact that many people began to respond to the messages, and hundreds, even thousands, of persons started going to El Cajas for the monthly First Saturday pilgrimages, indicates that the messages were received by many people. They are bearing fruit in their lives. The pilgrimages continue, and people speak of their "return to God" in their daily life.

In addition to the "public" messages, Mary also gave Patricia messages for specific individuals, as well as for herself. For the most part, I have confined the messages in this chapter to those for all of us.

The Holy Mother frequently addressed more than one topic in a single apparition message. Therefore, I have grouped the messages according to topics, excerpting those sections which fit the topic. However, each part of the message which I have quoted is complete for that topic within the message. I have been very careful not to "take a message out of context," thus guarding against the danger of changing the meaning of the message. Because Mary's own words are most profound, more beautiful than anything I could write, I have quoted them exactly from the English translations of the messages which Mary gave in Spanish.

A word of advice. As you read these messages, do so prayerfully. Hear Our Lady speaking to you. If you find your spirit moved by something you read, take it to heart and allow it to take root within you.

I Am the Guardian of the Faith

During the first visitation to Patricia the Holy Virgin called herself the "Guardian of the Faith." The name speaks the mission, and Mary was to use that title many times in the days and months that followed. Faith in Jesus Christ is being challenged on many fronts today, especially in Cuenca due to the promotion of Liberation Theology. The Holy Virgin, in her apparitions and in the messages she gave to Patricia and to us, is carrying out her mission to protect and guard our faith from the onslaught of false ideologies and confusing ways of thinking.

We are living in the last days of the second millennium, preparing for the third millennium of Our Lord Jesus Christ. Our world is torn with strife and sickness, with natural and man-made disasters, with the threat of world war, but, even more devastating, with a crisis of faith. The Catholic Church is being torn apart from within as well as from without. Theologians and cardinals, bishops and priests, religious and laity are challenging the Scriptures and the Tradition of our faith. Loyalty to Our Holy Father, the successor of St. Peter, for some is no longer an important part of their Catholic faith. "Individual rights" and "individual freedoms" have taken over the thought patterns of some of the most learned of scholars. The evil one is hard at work confusing and pulling apart, sowing seeds of disbelief and discord, attempting to take over the Holy Catholic Church through organizations and individuals who have fallen sway to his convincing arguments.

As we read and study Mary's messages we will discover in them the important dimension of faith.

On more than one occasion, The Holy Virgin asked for "faithful conversion from a humble heart." Throughout her messages she often refers to "faith." The following excerpts speak for themselves:

> I want all to be strong in their faith...Be an example, a faithful witness...Be the faithful reflection of my Son Jesus in the world...Today there is great confusion and tribulation of the faith...The times of darkness have begun, the darkness of your faith...The times of tribulation have begun, the tribulation of your faith...The darkness of faith of my little ones inhabits the world...Your faith is demonstrated not only in prayer but also in your actions.

Our Holy Mother wants all of her children to be happy in this world and to enjoy happiness with her in eternity. And so, she does not hesitate to speak a word that for some is difficult to hear; words of disasters and war, words of chastisements and confusion. Her role is to urge us to live the more difficult passages of the Scriptures so that we will bring others to conversion by our loving God and loving our neighbor as ourselves.

The Virgin Mother has explained her own mission to Patricia. She, as a good mother, is leading us to the Merciful Heart of her Son, Jesus Christ, so that we can receive His Divine Mercy. In a locution to Patricia in February 1991, The Holy Virgin compared herself to John the Baptist, who as the precursor of Jesus, announced His coming as Savior. She, in these days, is His precursor, announcing His coming as judge. Her messages detail for us the emphasis we should have on the things of God in our daily life.

Prayer

A study of the messages of all the Marian apparitions reveals that one message is consistent and primary to all the Holy Virgin's other specific messages: the invitation and call to prayer.

Jesus went off to the desert to pray. The disciples asked Jesus to teach them to pray. Communion with God is part of the nature of man. Because our relationship with God is the key to eternal life, Our Mother calls us to prayer.

> Pray much for peace in the world for it is now that it needs it the most.
>
> It is a time of prayer.
>
> My loved ones, little ones, my little souls, today I exhort you to prayer, peace and love; to share love with everyone.
>
> I ask all my little ones to be united in prayer.
>
> Little children, be humble, perseverant, and constant in prayer.

Peace seems to be Mary's primary concern for us. She explains that the peace she is speaking about rests in each of our hearts, and is the peace that only Jesus can give when we are in right relationship with God, with our brother, and with ourself. Now is the time to turn to Our Lord and Savior and be converted. Our prayer should reflect our relationship with God, and be the constant impetus for conversion. Mary encourages us to think about what we pray.

> Pray slowly because prayers said in a hurry do not reach heaven.

Obviously, prayers said in a hurry may not really be prayer. Prayer is communication with God. If we rush through our prayers, we might just be saying words, and we may not be communicating with God.

> Pray to me and I will keep you under my mantle and in the Heart of my Son.
>
> Now I am very happy to see the faith of my children when they sing and raise their prayers.
>
> I am smiling because you are being sincere in your prayers.
>
> You do not know how happy the Heart of my Son becomes when your prayers rise.
>
> Pray, pray and put into practice the Word.

Know that your little prayers are great in heaven.

I love you very much and my Son is pleased with your prayers.

Heaven rejoices when we are in touch with God. Mary desires to protect us under her mantle, and she asks us to pray in order to be there.

Penetrate more deeply in prayer.

Abandon yourselves more to prayer of contemplation.

All prayer is not words. Our Lady calls us to "ponder in our hearts" the Word of God, just as she did throughout her life.

I want you to have more prayer groups, that you learn how to pray and abandon yourselves in the Divine contemplation of your Beloved Heart, which is your Father.

Pray to me everyday because I will illumine your paths, my little souls.

Today you must pray more than ever because the time is short. Pray much.

Leave behind all the evil which surrounds you, all sin, continue on the path of prayer.

What We Should Be Praying For

The Virgin, through Patricia, tells us what we should be praying for. She encourages us all to live the Gospel life and to be examples for others, leading them to conversion:

"Pray, pray and put into practice the Word. Help those who need it. In this way, the just will be demanded more of than the unjust."

Pray that the Truth of the Father may shine in the world.

Pray much for peace in the world for it is now that it needs it the most.

Frequently, throughout her messages, Our Holy Mother conveys her love for all consecrated persons, especially for priests and sisters, and for the Holy Father. One of her frequent requests is that we pray for them.

> You must pray for an increase of religious sisters in the world, for more priests.

> Pray much for conversions in the whole world, for those children who have consecrated their life to the Father.

> Pray much for them (priests) because Satan is penetrating into the depths of the Holy Church.

> Now more than ever should you pray for priests. Do not judge my favorite sons.

> Priests, bishops are my chosen sons. You must pray a great deal for them.

> My little souls, pray much for my chosen and beloved son, my Pope.

Mary's call for peace centers around the conversion of souls. Sin is a reality in our world, and she calls us to turn away from sin, and turn back to God. We pray for her intentions when we pray against the sin in our world today: personal sin as well as the sins of the world in general.

> Humanity must pray and sacrifice in reparation for the sins of the world.

> Pray for the souls who roam around the world, pray for those who prefer an easy way.

> Pray for the children who have gone astray through the ways of evil.

> Pray much for those who are involved in drugs, alcohol and in music and those things which offend the heart of my Son.

> You must pray that there will be more peace in the hearts of the laity; that there be no drug addiction, or alcoholism; that there be no fashions that insult the Lord, nor music that insult my Son, Jesus. You must pray for the whole world, for those who do not want

to listen to the last calls from Heaven for you, the children of the Lord.

Pray for those who choose the easy way because it will not lead them to the same (easy) destiny.

We are so fortunate to have a Mother who reminds us that sickness and suffering, of all kinds, accepted in union with the sufferings of Jesus Christ, will bring us consolation in this world and joy in the next. As a loving Mother, she shares her concern for the sick and the suffering.

Pray for all the sick, for all the elderly, for all my little children who are frightened with events that are taking place.

Angels

Many people today have a renewed interest in angels. Others are not aware of the role of angels in their daily lives. Frequently, Mary appeared to Patricia accompanied by angels. She encourages us to take advantage of these protectors that God has provided for us. I frequently pray to my Guardian Angel. And always, before a pilgrimage, I ask God to assign a special angel to be our guardian and protector as we travel.

Pray to your Guardian Angel everyday that he protect you. Intercede to St. Michael the Archangel that you be not tempted by the devil, to Gabriel for truth.

Purgatory

In both our life and our death, Mary shows her concern for us. Frequently, in her apparition messages, she asks us to pray for the souls in purgatory, saying that they are waiting for our prayers. We need not worry if a person is in Purgatory or not. The treasury of the Church holds all our prayers, and if we pray for a particular person, and that person no longer needs our prayers, they go into the treasury of the Church for some soul who does need them. No prayer is lost.

Pray much for the souls in holy Purgatory.

Mary As Intercessor

And finally, Our Mother asks us to pray to her so that she can intercede for us to God, our Father. Mary recognizes her role in relation to our praying to her, and she asks us to allow her to fulfill one of her primary functions in heaven by praying to her. Of herself, she has no power. She takes our requests to God, and in turn brings us the graces He desires to give us.

Pray to me in order to obtain your requests from my son, Jesus.

How Should We Pray

As a mother, Mary has every person's well being at heart. She knows our weaknesses and our desires. She wants a people united in the love of her Son, Jesus Christ. She asks us to be concerned about our brothers and sisters, and to pray for them. Our Holy Mother is specific in calling us to many forms of prayer.

Abandon yourselves more to prayer of contemplation.

Receive Communion, go to confession, visit the Blessed Sacrament.

Pray the Angelus, go to Mass frequently, not just on Sundays.

Pray much in this month of May. Make prayer chains with the Angelus, the Rosary, daily Mass, for this will help that your faith be not confused and that evil will not penetrate your country.

I ask that you pray the Rosary as a family, daily, with lively faith, with simple hearts.

Everyday pray the fifteen sacred mysteries of the Rosary.

The Rosary

There is no question that Mary's favorite prayer is the Rosary. Many, many times she called for the praying of the complete Rosary, and daily. She told Patricia that for some it is too difficult to pray the fifteen decades all at once. Therefore, they should spread it out over the day, praying the Joyful Mysteries in the morning, the Sorrowful Mysteries in the middle of the day and the Glorious Mysteries in the evening. How our Mother understands us!

Mary is also aware that some people have difficulty praying the Rosary and therefore don't pray it at all. The Holy Virgin knows better than we the value of the Rosary and she asks us to pray it in faith, without understanding why. Just do it, she begs. She said:

> The Rosary is the most complete prayer. Do not ask yourself why you pray it. Let it be your shield against the evil one who is acting. Do not detach yourselves of it.

Most Complete Prayer

Some people question the statement, "The Rosary is the most complete prayer." The Holy Virgin has explained that when we pray the fifteen decades of the Rosary, we meditate on the key events in the whole life of Jesus and in her life. In this sense, the Rosary is "the most complete prayer" for we recall the saving acts of Jesus from his birth to his Ascension into Heaven, and then his actions there, sending the Holy Spirit, calling his Mother home, and crowning her Queen of Heaven and earth. Her messages give us insight into the value of the Rosary and why we should pray it everyday.

> Pray the Rosary, which is a shield against evil.
>
> . . .the Rosary, which is the imprint of God's love.
>
> The Rosary is the most complete prayer.
>
> The Rosary is a very powerful weapon which could be used to remove the forces of the devil in this world.
>
> The most powerful weapon, the Rosary, will combat all evil, do not detach yourself of this weapon.
>
> . . .the Holy Rosary, the preferred prayer of my chosen one, the Pope.

We noticed that many people in Cuenca were wearing the Rosary around their necks, not like a string of pearls, but under their shirts or blouses, much like a scapular. Many were also wearing the scapular. Often, the rosaries were simple ones made of cord, knotted to form the beads. The people were wearing them in response to a directive from Our Lady who said:

> Wear always this Rosary on you which will protect you against evil.
>
> Lift up your rosaries as I have asked you before. Do not be so slow to listen to me. I don't want you to take off your necks this sign which will be the sign of your salvation. Use the holy Scapular, the holy Rosary, your blessed medals. Do not allow Satan to impede you from using them because they will be a great sign of your protection.

Holy Mass and the Eucharist

There is no substitute for Holy Mass. It is the most perfect of prayers. In many of her messages to Patricia, the Holy Virgin urged us to participate in Holy Mass as frequently as possible, even daily, saying often, "Go to daily Mass," or "Go often to Mass, besides Sunday."

Eucharist, the body and blood of Jesus Christ, is the food our souls need. Mary spoke about her concern for the lack of reverence for the Eucharist, manifested in the way people dress when they go to Mass, not being respectful of their own bodies, or where they are going, or in whose presence they will be. She also spoke of the disrespect for the Eucharist by those who receive it in their hands, but do not consume it. Rather, they take the Sacred Body of Jesus for Satanic rituals. In some countries and areas this practice is more prevalent than in others.

> These are some of the victories in the world. The Sacred Body of my Son, when it is distributed at Mass, is no longer given from the priest's hand into the mouth of the faithful. But the faithful take the Sacred Body of my Son with their hands, and know then, my

little ones, that now, by many in the world, it is used for Satanic rituals.

We asked Patricia if Mary had ever said anything about Vatican II, and her response was an emphatic "Yes." The Holy Virgin said we must obey Vatican II, but that many abuses have crept into Church practices because of the way some of the changes of Vatican II have been interpreted. Here, Mary is not speaking against Communion in the hand, but against the ease with which some people can now obtain the consecrated host for Satanic purposes.

Go to Mass and visit the Blessed Sacrament.

I want you to go to Mass not only on Sundays. I need more from you, my little ones.

Another great victory (for Satan) are fashions, and the way young women go dressed to Mass, obscene. They arouse temptation and sin. They should be respectful and dress in a way in which they will not be looked at sinfully, but rather with honesty and respect.

Adoration of the Blessed Sacrament

The Eucharist is central to the life of a Catholic and Mary knows how much we need Jesus. "Visit the Blessed Sacrament often." In the presence of the Blessed Sacrament, at the foot of the Cross, we will find all that we need for our lives—knowledge of the will of God, direction, inspiration, encouragement, consolation, and the merciful love of Jesus. When we humble ourselves before him and bow down in lowly adoration, he picks us up and gives us the grace to live as his faithful followers.

Be an example, youth, an example of peace, of holiness, pray the Rosary, go to daily Mass, visit the Blessed Sacrament, pray the Angelus, pray in family, do penance, mortification, fasting.

My tears are poured out for the evil that exists in the world, through atheism and materialism, through adoring false gods, through ignoring the Word of God and the Sacraments.

Penance and Fasting

The early Fathers of the Church taught that prayer, fasting and works of mercy were necessary for us to grow in holiness. Mary has often called us to prayer, to fasting, and to works of mercy, saying:

> Do penance and fast, and with prayer you will reach the heart of my Son.
>
> You must fast at least once a week.
>
> Fast on bread and water at least once a week.
>
> I want Thursdays to be a day of fasting on bread and water.

When Patricia told us that the Virgin had requested a bread and water fast on Thursdays, we gasped. In Marian apparitions in other places, Wednesday and Fridays have been requested as fast days. ''Wednesday, Thursday, Friday,'' we voiced. ''No,'' Patricia replied, ''just one day a week is what the Holy Virgin requests. Two, if possible.'' We realize, of course, that the day is not important; rather the important thing is that we fast one day as our Mother has requested.

> Tell them that I love them much and I need their prayer, fasting and penance.
>
> Repent, fast, do penance.
>
> I need your conversion my little one, I need more of your prayer, penance and fasting...

Why fast and do penance? Jesus tells us that some things can only be done with prayer and fasting. Spiritual masters teach us that penance, mortification and fasting are necessary, not only for personal holiness, but to open the flood gates of the Father's merciful love in particular situations. The Holy Virgin attests to this power when she says:

> Your prayers, penances, and fasts are helping to deter the determination of the Third World War.
>
> You, my little souls, do you forget that with prayer and fasting you can deter wars and natural catastrophes?

> I need your prayer, fasting and penance. Contribute to your salvation.
>
> My daughter, I ask of you repentance, fasting and penance. Your daughter will be healed, but you must change.
>
> Parents be conscious that you will achieve much more from your children with prayer, penance, and fasting than with your words and sermons, because these will fall on deaf ears.
>
> Fast today, Thursdays, because with fasting all the problems will change.
>
> . . . because with prayer, penance, mortification and fasting many souls in the world can be saved.
>
> Your prayers, your fastings, cause so much joy to my heart.

Do we need any other motivation to begin to fast? Our ultimate goal should be bread and water fasting, but our initial entry into the penance of fasting may have to be something much less. Prudence must dominate. Just as Our Lady tells us to spread out the praying of the Rosary throughout the day, so she tells us to begin to fast. That's the important thing. Begin to fast and allow God, who sees the intentions of the heart, to give us the grace to advance to the "best fast," bread and water. It may take a lifetime, and that is all right. The traditional fasting which the Church recommends is a good place to start.

Works of Mercy

In addition to prayer and fasting, works of mercy complete the threefold requirements for growing in the spiritual life and for becoming more like Jesus and Mary. Early in her visitations to Patricia, the Holy Virgin spoke of her desire that we include works of mercy in our daily life. She instructed the young people who gathered regularly to pray the Rosary:

> I would like that in the place where you pray there be the "wardrobe for the poor" and that food be collected for the poor. Children, do not abandon those

> who have nothing to eat or to wear, because in them is the kingdom of heaven. See in them your Father, Son, and Spirit, and I will keep you under my mantle.
>
> Be united, love your brothers, fulfill the works of mercy, my little ones.
>
> Do works of mercy among lonely people, visit the elderly, the sick.
>
> Help those who are of most need, the poor of heart, the materially poor, because in the hungry, in the thirsty, in the naked, in the imprisoned is my Son Jesus.
>
> . . . give alms in the temple of your Father.
>
> Only a little bit of your love, only that do I ask of you. Visit the sick, help those who are victims of the floods. You have much work, my children, for those poor hearts enriched by the glory of God.
>
> I ask that you share love with those who do not have it, joy with those who are sad, that you give consolation to those who are grieved. Children, practice charity and love.

We see that Our Lady blesses us when we visit the elderly and clothe the naked. She promises to keep us under her sacred mantle, protecting us and drawing us closer to herself. There should be no question as to how we are to live out the second Great Commandment: Love your neighbor as yourself. Unfortunately, many of us put off doing good works until there is some disaster or crisis. Then we rally round the cause. Rather, we are called to incorporate the spiritual and corporal works of mercy into our daily life if, in the eternal kingdom, we want to hear the words, "What you did for the least of these, you did to me. Enter into the joy of the Lord."

Responsibilities of Parents

Family is God's idea, not man's. The way of Jesus is the family. He chose to be born into a family, and he calls each of us to be part of his family. Today, possibly more than ever in the history of mankind, family life is being challenged, and because of its important role in the salvation of souls, the Holy Virgin spoke about the responsibility parents have to bring up their children in the ways of God. She is keenly aware of those things which challenge parental authority and the pressures young people are exposed to today. Nothing escapes her motherly knowledge and wisdom.

> Parents, do not allow your children to be lost in evil. Pray much for those who are involved in drugs, alcohol and in music and those things which offend the heart of my Son.
>
> Tell this message to parents. They must take care, specially, with their children. Parents should be an example of life; they must know how to live righteous lives.
>
> Tell parents not to offer too much freedom to their children, because this freedom is the reason my little ones become victims of the tricks of Satan.
>
> Tell parents that they should not allow their children to listen to that music which insults Our Blessed Father.
>
> Tell parents that there should be less television, that all must be censored by parents. Be careful of your teenagers.
>
> Tell parents to encourage their children to prayer in the family, especially the holy Rosary, to penance, fasting, that they go to confession, communion, sacrifice, show them firmness, uprightness with love, and act in this way.
>
> Parents be conscious that you will achieve much more from your children with prayer, penance, fasting than with your words and sermons, because these will fall on deaf ears.
>
> Little children, be an example of love to your parents. Parents teach Love. Teach purity and goodness.

The Role of Satan in Our World Today

The role of Satan and his influence in our world today is minimized or denied by many. Our Holy Mother tells us otherwise, saying that Satan is "very active" today, trying to convince us to go his way rather than that way which will lead us to eternal glory. We are easily influenced by what we see and what we hear. Satan, being the master of deceit and confusion, is daily carrying out his mission to twist our thinking and to cause us to accept practices today that in the past were scandalous. Our holy Mother spoke of the "victories" of Satan in our world today.

> . . . for there is a hell as there is a heaven, but there is only one King, God the Father; for Satan exists who contains hatred, perversion and all that does not give peace to your hearts.
>
> My children, give your hearts over; do not allow Satan to penetrate your heart. Fight against evil and give your heart to the Sacred Heart of my Son and to my Immaculate Heart.
>
> And all that I tell you is in Sacred Scripture. Fulfill what I ask of you. Diabolic trends, and there are many in the world, try to affect and entangle my little souls. Satan will reach the summit, being adored by my children. His images will be idolized. A false prophet exists who will entangle them saying that he is God, but he is from the blood of the demon. He will betray the Father. And the one who has the heart and wisdom will realize that he (the false prophet) carries the number of the beast, "666" on his right hand. Satan is set loose to touch my little ones, but I am that woman whom the Father announced, who will crush the head of the serpent that is Satan.
>
> Pray much for them (priests) because Satan is penetrating into the depths of the Holy Church.
>
> Do not let Satan penetrate you. I am the Guardian of the Faith.
>
> My children, Satan wants to destroy the missions which heaven has granted you, children of the light. In the same way he will try to destroy the church, but his attempts will be in vain if you convert.

. . . and so Satan has penetrated in the very depths of the Holy Church. But do not judge those who judge you. Respect priests no matter how mistaken they could be, even though (sic) some of them have children after having consecrated their life and their chastity for the rest of their days; where many do not fulfill the way of life they offered to the Father.

Another of Satan's victories is that young women, my little ones, give themselves to men before marriage. They have no right, for the body and the soul belong to God and they may do it only if He allows it through the Blessed Sacrament (of Marriage), because what God unites man cannot separate.

Another great victory of Satan is divorce. Those who fail in one of the greatest blessings, matrimony, having many lovers and try to separate and divide that which the Father has united.

Another great victory is abortion, which is an attempt against the great blessing of the Father, life.

Another great victory of Satan are fashions, styles, and the way young women dress for Mass, obscenely. They arouse temptation to sin. They should be respectful and dress in a way in which they will not be looked at sinfully, rather with honesty and respect.

For you know that fashions and music are a great victory for Satan. For, with fashions he moves people to become slaves of money and of sin. For those who exhibit their body, and who do not repent, will be judged, because the Father did not give the body to be exhibited, but to take care of it as a temple of God. For you know that fashions are encouragement for Satan to dress himself in their feminine form. That music, in how many messages I have asked you to abandon it, for you know they are praises to Satan and they will remain engraved in your mind, for he infuses them and they will remain engraved in your life. He, through this music, makes mockery of the Father, of my beloved Son, and of the Spirit of God, and of me, his mother. His great victory is to be idolized to the point of offering rituals with human blood and other human elements and (they) have even offered the sacrifice of their life in order to give their soul to Satan. He has managed that images be made to adore him, and they have their book which they say is sacred, for they have great temples for his adoration.

Improper deeds take place with drugs which promote sexual scenes with children who are forced by Satanists. . .for he sees to it that they get drugged, or drunk. . . .For he will try to involve them with sin, with vain pleasures, even with their physical beauty. He will try to make them feel that he will make their body, which should be the temple of God, his temple. That is, he will make some believe only in themselves and in no one else, and they will not want to look at their soul but they will look only at their physical appearance.

Satan will entangle you, do not allow him to confuse you. Do not allow him to take my Son's place.

I exhort you to peace. Lift up your rosaries as I have asked you before. Do not be so slow to listen to me. I don't want you to take off your necks this sign which will be the sign of your salvation. Use the holy Scapular, the holy Rosary, your blessed medals. Do not allow Satan to stop you from using them because they will be a great sign of your protection. Have holy water in your homes.

These are some of the many victories of that announced beast. You know that you should have your eyes wide open in order to differentiate and not allow yourselves to be confused between pleasure, and sacrifice and truth. I only want that you seek holiness in your words and in your actions, for only the Father, my Son, and the Spirit of God, and myself your Mother, know what you think, feel and do. But Satan doesn't. He only knows how you act. That is what you can do and cannot do. So, do not allow him to reach you in your weakest parts. For I do not want you that way but pure, sure and strong in your faith.

Satan is especially active among the youth today. They are the future church, and he would try to destroy them while they are still young and able to be formed.

> (Parents) Use discipline, patience, love. Educate your children with the example of your own life. Never before has Satan been seen working so hard among the youth; how my dear youth walk, confused and blinded without any desire to change or even to attempt it.
>
> My daughter, Satan's hand is in the youth, you must take Satan's hand off and put the hand of my Son upon the hearts of the whole world.
>
> My daughter, now more than ever is Satan acting among your young women and young men, do not allow sin to enter them. Satan will try to inspire their fashions, he will try to make them captives of his monstrous work.
>
> To my youthful sinners, those who open today their heart to God the Father. Youth, little children, today Satan has wrapped you in sin, prostitution, alcohol, drugs, sex. My children, take off the hand of Satan and put the hand of my Son Jesus in your hearts. Be an example, youth, an example of peace, of holiness, pray the Rosary, go to daily Mass, visit the Blessed Sacrament, pray the Angelus, pray in family, do penance, mortification, fasting.

The Merciful Heart of Jesus

The Holy Virgin spoke often about the Merciful Heart of her Son, Jesus. She said we were living in the time of the Mercy of God, "Know, children, that you are living in the time of the Mercy of the Father, of my beloved Son, and of the Spirit of God in the world."

Today, more than ever before, we need God's mercy. Today is the time of mercy, Divine Mercy. The Merciful Heart of Jesus is our refuge, our strength, our consolation, and our encouragement.

Patricia was doubly blessed because throughout the period in which she received the heavenly visitations of Mary, Jesus would also appear to her, presenting himself with red and white rays of grace emanating from his heart. The Merciful Heart of Jesus!

The first time Jesus appeared to her was on December 27, 1988, in the Chapel of the Madres Catalinas in San Roque. The next day, Jesus appeared again and Patricia described what she saw: "The Lord is standing on a cloud, barefooted. He has a white tunic and from His heart come forth two rays, one white, another red. He has big, long, honey colored eyes. His skin is golden and he has a beard. His hair is long and brown. He has his arms extended and he has the wounds on his feet and hands. Just as the Virgin, He speaks with only a slight Spanish accent. His voice is smooth, sweet, and very deep."

At that time, Jesus spoke the following message to Patricia:

> I would want that out of your mission you make a song of joy. I want you not to be saddened, but joyful because I am joyful. Do not fear, daughters.
>
> Be patient, tranquil. Do not run, because without thinking you get nothing, you may fall. Do not be so proper. Do not look after your good alone. Give yourselves over to my will. All that I say to you is because I look for something in you and everything is said. The time is short and there are no buts. It will be a hard and arduous mission and I will compensate you with my salvation.
>
> Know that He who speaks to you is your brother, Jesus Christ. Why do you sometimes doubt my presence? I have spoken to you many times, but my little souls, you are innocent in Divine Wisdom. Love my Mother because she holds back the fury of heaven. Love her in all the good that happens to you and keep much discretion.
>
> I am the Merciful Jesus, I am great in heart. Ask, children. I would like the day of my Mercy to be celebrated. Have in your homes an image of my Merciful Heart.

Do not forget that the Father is good and that I came to the world for you, my beloved ones.

I am Jesus and know it, for all is in your hands. The time is short, and I am already very wounded with all that my stray children have done. I love you, my chosen ones.

On Good Friday, March 24, 1989, Jesus appeared to Patricia and said:

My children, I am great in love; my Heart is inclined to help you for forgiveness. I am the Divine Mercy of the Father who came to the world for your salvation.

On Easter Sunday, Jesus appeared again to Patricia and said:

Be then faithful, for I will not leave you. My heart is happy to see how you pray the Novena of my Mercy...

Again on April 2, 1989, the Second Sunday of Easter, Jesus appeared to Patricia and said:

Today is the day of my Mercy. You do not know that my heart is big. I want to help you, my little ones; ask, my children. This day is Universal because I am universal.

The celebration of the Feast of Divine Mercy on the Second Sunday of Easter (formerly called Low Sunday) has not been promulgated by the Catholic Church at this time. However, it is celebrated privately by many in response to the message of mercy made known by Sr. Faustina of Poland.

Jesus went on to say:

Those of you who have come out of love and unselfishly, these will be blessed, and those who have come today out of interest and curiosity, these will suffer. My Love is great and I do not desire that you suffer, nor that your hearts be oppressed by pain. I am the Merciful Jesus, and I am always with my Mother. I have not come to the world in vain; I came to the world for your salvation. I love you much. Practice the message of love, of peace and of humility; pray to my Mother, because in this way you pray with me. Pray the holy

Rosary because you remember my life, that of God made man, together with my most pure Mother. Goodbye.

The Holy Virgin also spoke to Patricia about the Merciful Heart of Jesus encouraging us to have an image of the Merciful Heart of Jesus and of her Immaculate Heart in our homes:

> My daughters, I love you much. I am smiling as I see how my daughters pray. Keep yourselves in my Immaculate Heart and in the Merciful Heart of my Son. He is sad to see that His message does not reach these little hearts.
>
> You are in the cradle in the mercy of my Son, my little ones. Do not be afraid, my dear ones. Know that your little prayers are great in heaven.
>
> Blessings to those children of mine who in their homes keep an altar with a crucifix of my blessed Son, an image of the Heart of my Son and His mercy, as well as an image of my Immaculate Heart, and holy water.
>
> Love the Heart of my Son and His Mercy and love my Immaculate Heart.

The Great Secret

The Holy Virgin gave Patricia the great secret when she appeared to her in the Church on Tepeyac, Guadalupe, Mexico in October, 1988. Our Lady said it corresponds to the one given to other visionaries throughout the world. Patricia was able to tell us, "She gave me the secret that there are bad things going to happen in the world, and what is asked for is conversion. I asked her if I could tell everybody about the secret and the Virgin said, 'No,' because it was too strong a message to give and it would create panic. And so, I said, I can't just forget about this. And the Virgin said, 'One month ahead of time I'll tell you so you can say.' " Patricia has not said anymore about the timing of the secret, and since it is part of the secret, she won't talk about it.

At a later time, the Virgin told Patricia certain parts of the secret could be revealed. In fact, the Great Secret that the Virgin gave Patricia contains three parts. Patricia told us that all three parts have something to do with future events which will be chastisements for our world. Our Lady spoke several times about the possibility of a third world war, of natural disasters and man-made disasters:

> Little children, know that all that you do benefits the world. Your prayers, penances, and fasts are helping to deter the determination of the third World War. Everything is as I have said before. It is in your hands. It depends on you whether the chastisement be as strong as the sorrow that my Son feels or that it (the chastisement) be appeased with prayer.
>
> Fast on bread and water at least once a week. Pray the Rosary daily. You, my little souls, do you forget that with prayer and fasting you can deter wars and natural catastrophes?
>
> Children, you will suffer much, the path is hard, but the recompense will be salvation. Children, I love you from the heart, I am your Mother, my children, my little souls, the greatest sinners. Repent of all evil that you have committed. Children, it is a time of purification of souls. The path is short.
>
> My loved ones, children, the third World War threatens the world. Today, more than ever, I ask prayer of you. . . . Transmit the peace of my Son Jesus, because great catastrophes are coming upon humanity. Today, children, I am present and I protect you under my mantle. I have picked up your faith and I have made of it a beautiful rose of peace.
>
> Great catastrophes are coming upon humanity; the third world war threatens the world. Natural catastrophes created by man are coming. You must be strong with a faith that is like a rock.
>
> Children, there is much sorrow in my heart, for many natural catastrophes and others created by man are coming. Hard times are already taking place, a short

decade filled with suffering. The third world war is near. Do not frighten your hearts, because the peace of God is with you.

Third World War

The mention of a third world war causes concern. The Holy Virgin told Patricia that one is near, if we do not convert, fast and pray. We seem to have a choice.

Nevertheless, the Virgin did tell Patricia some details about such a war which she was allowed to share with us. We listened intently as she said, "The war is near. It will be started with false peace treaties, treaties in which we should not place our trust. Many countries would be involved, among them China, Rumania, Russia, and the United States. Initially Poland will be involved also, but when the Holy Father leaves Rome, going first to France and then to Poland, Poland would be protected." As we sat in silence, looking at Patricia, she said, "That is why conversion now is so important."

> Little children, know that all that you do benefits the world. Your prayers, penances, and fasts are helping to prevent the third World War. Everything is as I have told you. All is in your hands. From you it depends whether the chastisement will be as strong as the pain that my Son feels or that the chastisement be diminished with prayer.
>
> You know, my daughter, that the third nuclear war is near. Pray, my children, for China, Russia, Czechoslovakia. Pray for the countries from the South. Catastrophes come there. Pray for Panama, Nicaragua, El Salvador. Repent, fast, make penance....Tell them that I love them so much, all of them.
>
> ...my son. You have to help very much my little daughter. My daughter is going to suffer very, very much as the time is short. The third world war is near, natural catastrophes, earthquakes, floods such as humanity has never seen before because of so much sin in the world. You know that you are surrounded by much sin. Convert your heart. Give it to me. Have peace.

Pray much for the countries of Latin America. Pray very much for the countries of Central America. Pray for the Soviet Union, Russia, the United States, Czechoslovakia, and China. These are countries that will be involved in the third world war.

Great times of tribulation are coming. Natural catastrophes and those created by men, and the third world war are near. You should keep these in your heart. You should pray for the Holy Father, my Pope, my chosen son. You should pray for priests, the bishops and members of the clergy. You should pray for the wounds which you cause the heart of my son Jesus.

My little children, little ones, I am your Mother from heaven, the Holy Mary, always Virgin. You who are all gathered in faith, my loved ones, children, the third world war threatens the world. Today, more than ever, I ask you for prayer. Transmit the peace of my Son, Jesus, because great catastrophes are coming upon humanity. Today, children, I am present and I am protecting you under my mantle. I have gathered up your faith and I have made of it a beautiful rose of peace.

Days of Darkness

Days of darkness are spoken about in the Book of Revelations. The Holy Virgin also spoke about them saying that the earth would go out of its orbit for three days. At that time, the second coming of Jesus will be near. The devil will take over the world. During those days, families should be in continuous prayer. Because of false prophets, who will falsify the Words of Christ, we have to be in the state of grace so we can discern the good from the evil. We have to have the flame of Jesus Christ in our soul. We should not open the door of our homes to anybody. We are simply to keep on praying. The Virgin said it would be better not even to look through the window because we will see the justice of God over the people. It will be so terrible, that we will not want to see it.

We asked Patricia if she had ever read about these things, or if she was familiar with the messages of other reported apparitions of Our Lady such as those in Akita, Japan; Medugorje, Jugoslavia; or Kibeho, Africa. Was she familiar with Fr. Gobbi and the Marian Movement of Priests?

Her response was simple and manifested great wisdom, "Before the apparitions, I had never heard nor read about them, but now people have given me many books, but I don't want to read them. I don't want to hear anything about any other place because I don't want to get confused now." She said she had been told by a priest about Fr. Gobbi, but had never read any of the messages. When I was in Rome with Patricia, she told me that once a woman had brought a video about the apparitions in Medugorje, Jugoslavia, to her school, but she had walked out of it, saying, "How ridiculous!"

Everything Patricia had told us, has been said before either in Scripture, or in revelations of other reported apparitions or those approved by the Church, or by mystics or prophets in the Church. Our Lady was not revealing anything new. What amazed us was that it all seemed to come together here in the Holy Virgin's messages to Patricia. We had heard it all before, in pieces; but here it seemed as if the message was more complete.

Conversion: Faithful Conversion

Our Mother asks us for faithful conversion, now. She continuously reminds us that through conversion, prayer and fasting we can hold back the hand of God. The important thing is not to panic, or not to convert out of fear, but to convert and to change our lives because that is what we should be doing anyway. After the message from Mary at Fatima, many people began to pray the Rosary, making the First Saturdays, and wearing the scapular. Yet, we had another war, World War II. Why? Was it because there were not "faithful conversions"? Did people pray out of fear, and not from a changed heart? I believe that happened, and so we had another world war. The hand of God was not held back because there were not enough faithful conversions. Now, once again, our Mother is being sent by our loving Father, to call us back to himself in "faithful conversion." It is all in our hands.

The Virgin Mary repeatedly reminds us that our prayers and penances, fasting and good works do make a difference. She often reminds us that we should not fear the chastisements or even another world war, if the peace of God is in our hearts. We are asked to "sow joy" and to live under Mary's protective mantle. "Faithful conversion from a humble heart," is the way Patricia explained it. Our Lady said:

> Take a good look at where it is that you are going. I ask of you faithful conversion.
>
> Today I ask that your decision be faithful, that you decide to live the callings which have been given. I desire that you should be active in living out and communicating my messages.
>
> Little children, I need speedy conversion, prayer; more than anything, a faithful conversion from a humble heart.
>
> Why do you take so long to change; do not leave to tomorrow what you can do today. Begin today with firm steps towards a faithful conversion, a conversion of love. Children, I am happy to see many sensitive souls, but don't cover the soul with a mask of hatred, resentment, pride. Remove the cancer of pride because it is killing your souls. Forgive, my little children, my loved ones. I fill your heart with grace. I fill you with love. I fill you with peace, little children.
>
> All that I have told you is because God the Father has asked me to. Children, the time is short, very short. Conversion must be faithful. Remove all evil sentiments because Satan penetrates in them. Remove them with the Presence of God in your souls. Children, give thanks to God for what you have.

Guardian Angels

We asked Patricia if angels ever accompanied the Holy Virgin. "On some occasions," she responded, smiling and tilting her head backwards slightly, obviously recalling some pleasant experience. The Holy Virgin identified those who accompanied her as the Archangels Michael, Gabriel and Raphael, saying:

> My children, I exhort you to peace, to the love of my Son Jesus who is present here, together with the Archangels Michael and Raphael, my protectors.

And on another occasion, the Virgin said,

> Today, I am accompanied by the Archangels, St. Michael and St. Gabriel. They are my protectors. You must pray to your Guardian Angel everyday that he protect you. Intercede to St. Michael the Archangel so that you will not be tempted by the devil, and to Gabriel for truth.

Patricia told us that the Holy Virgin's Guardian Angel is St. Michael, the Archangel. And, when the Virgin encouraged Patricia to pray often to her own Guardian Angel, Patricia expressed a wish to see her Guardian Angel. Patricia smiled as she told us, ''He is a black angel.''

Of course, we wanted to know what the angels looked like, since angels are pure spirits and don't have bodies. ''Like little children. Sometimes they are completely naked, like little kids.'' Now, it was our turn to smile. How kind of God to allow the angels to be visible in just the way angels are often depicted in the famous masterpieces by the renowned artists.

Patricia said that sometimes the archangel Gabriel has a flower, a lily like St. Joseph, and a Rosary in his hands and Rafael often carries a book and a Rosary. The archangel Michael usually has a sword and the Rosary. The flower, the book, and the sword symbolize the primary mission of each archangel.

On October 3, 1989, Saint Michael, the Archangel presented himself to Patricia, who was with a group of young people, telling her that the youth must carry the cross that lies on their chests and they should wear a wooden crucifix as a symbol. The Blessed Virgin did not appear at this time, and the archangel told Patricia to be tranquil and reminded her that the Virgin loves her. He went on to say that she would see the Virgin only when the Blessed Virgin called her and not whenever Patricia wanted to see her.

Heaven, Hell and Purgatory

"Has the Virgin told you anything about heaven, hell or purgatory? Visionaries in other places have seen them; have you?" These questions followed naturally in our interview as we sought to learn everything about what Patricia had experienced. Nodding her head in the affirmative, Patricia responded, "The Virgin said that hell does exist, even though many people don't believe in it. That is why we need conversion, so we can save our souls and not receive the punishment of not seeing God."

"Once, when I was praying late into the night, the Holy Virgin appeared to me and said:

> My little one, I have kept you awake because I need to tell you and show you many things. Now I have told you before, the time is short, because you know there is condemnation for those who do not fulfill what God asks of them in His law. . . . For there is a hell as there is a heaven, but there is only one King, God the Father; for Satan exists who contains hatred, perversion and all that does not give peace to your hearts.

Patricia described hell as "a terrible place, like a big volcano where you see souls that hate each other. There are skulls and they don't have faces, but they hate and insult God. What are those little hats the bishops use? I could see some of those in hell."

Purgatory, she said, was like coming out of the volcano. She saw hands reaching out and crying, trying to get out. "And while I was there, I heard a voice telling me to pray for them because they couldn't do anything without our help."

On the Feast of Our Lady of Mount Carmel, July 16, the Virgin said, ". . . Today intercede that the souls in Purgatory be released, those that are a step away from coming out . . ."

She exhorted us to, "Pray much for the souls in holy Purgatory. Pray much for those who wander around the world. Pray for the elderly, pray for the sick."

Our penances, prayers, and sacrifices can benefit the souls in Purgatory. After a difficult procession up the mountain to El Cajas, the Virgin said, "...The procession has saved many souls from Purgatory..."

And heaven, Patricia said, "I didn't go in because I didn't deserve it. There were two choirs of angels at each side of the door. The Rosary, prayer, is the door, and the cross of the Rosary is the key to open the door to go into heaven." Patricia explained that prayer takes us to Jesus, who is the way, the truth and the life, and the cross that we carry over our back, our sufferings, is the key to open the door into heaven.

CHAPTER SEVENTEEN

PERSONAL EXPERIENCES

Our First Visit To El Cajas

For the three of us, it was our first visit to Ecuador. Fr., Angelus had been a missionary in Brazil, and Fr. Michael had visited Brazil to preach a retreat, but the West Coast of South America was new for all of us. We found a beautiful country, and beautiful people who love the Lord and his Mother, and who opened their hearts and homes to us. After a brief stay in Quito, we flew to Cuenca, in the southern part of the country, flying over many volcanic mountains.

On Friday morning, February 2, 1990, we visited with Patricia and her family. Then, Gaston took us to El Cajas. Along the way we passed many Indian families, walking, carrying their supplies, and their babies, on their backs. As we climbed higher and higher, the weather began to change. It got colder and even rained a little. Our first sight of the region of El Cajas which Our Lady had selected for the place of her apparitions was breathtaking. It was still natural and, for the most part, untainted by human constructions of buildings, roads, or paved paths. A few wooden bridges had been put in to make passing through the wider mountain streams easier and safer. There were a few people in the Garden area, adorning it with flowers.

The Geological Team

Among the people we met were a geological team who recounted some of the experiments they have been conducting before, during, and after the apparitions. These same kinds of radiation and magnetic wave tests have been done in other places of reported apparitions. Coming from a scientific background, having taught high school physics for many years, I was fascinated as they told us of the temperature differential inside the Garden and outside it during the apparition times. Inside was much warmer than outside the Garden.

The second fact that interested me was their observation of the movement of an ordinary compass. During the apparition, the compass needle rotated ninety degrees, pointing in the direction of the place where Patricia reports the Virgin appeared to her. It was not difficult for me to believe that the rotation happened. However, when we returned in March, I took a small compass with me and placed it on top of a huge bouquet of flowers when I knelt down in preparation for the apparition of Our Lady to Patricia. I had no difficulty zeroing it to the north, which was directly in front of me. From time to time I would glance down at it, and the needle was always stationary. During the time of apparition, I glanced at it, and I saw the compass needle rapidly rotating, first in one direction and then in the other direction. I immediately looked around to see if there was anything different in the vicinity which could have been responsible for the rotation. There was nothing. I had no explanation for the rotation. But, I do know how difficult it is to cause a magnetic compass to rotate through three hundred sixty degrees, first in one direction and then in the other. There had to be some invisible presence which caused the rapid rotation!

The next day when Patricia described the heavenly scene, telling us that Mary was accompanied by seven angels, I began to wonder if the angels might not have caused the rapid rotation of my compass. Of course, there is no way to test that theory, but, for me, there is no need to do so.

The Vigil

Friday evening, February 2, 1990, we participated in the celebration of Mass for the Feast of the Presentation of Our Lord, also known as Candlemas Day. Following Mass, dinner, and a change into our winter clothes, we began the ride to El Cajas with Gaston, his wife, Anita, and Bernardita, to spend the night in vigil as the Holy Mother had requested. It seemed as if we had only gone a short distance up the mountain when the traffic stopped. There were so many vehicles that the road was impassable. Cars, trucks, vans and buses were parked everywhere along the road, making it impossible to proceed. We were told that our only course of action was to walk. How far were we from the Garden? About ten miles! We started, joining thousands of other people who had also begun the long trek up the mountain.

We did indeed make the trip successfully, with no incidents of sickness or even feeling faint with the change of altitude. I knew that had to be a special grace from God, because our bodies were not yet acclimated to the high altitude. There was an old house nearby, now used as a tool shed, that we had been told we could go to. We were surprised to find it filled with other people who had also walked up the mountain. Patricia had gone into one room to rest, as she had not been feeling well for several days. She had walked up the mountain with us, and she knew Our Lady would wake her to tell her when to go to the Garden.

We found places on a bench along one wall. The only light came from a small kerosene heater in the middle of the room. It was impossible to sleep, as people moved in and out, frequently bumping against a huge pipe in the middle of the room. After some time, the fumes from the kerosene heater got the best of us, and we went outside. It was cold and it had begun to rain. One of the geologists had offered us the use of his tent. After some time, we found it and, along with Patricia's mother, went inside until the first signs of daybreak. It was dark, and we had no idea who else was there. The entry room was vacant, and that is where we tried to get some sleep. But, it was virtually impossible to do so. We tried to pray, but that was difficult also.

As the sun rose over the mountain, and we were able to see the area, we were amazed to see the wide expanse of people who had spent the night on the mountainside, without any covering to protect themselves from the cold wind and the rain. The local authorities estimated the crowd at one hundred eighteen thousand people. I had never seen so many people gathered together in one place.

Fr. Michael and I, and the people we were with from Quito, managed to get to the Garden area where we found Fr. Angelus, who had spent the night standing up in the Garden. He had become separated from us when Gaston, knowing that Fr. Angelus had a heart condition, put him on the back of his son's motorcycle for the ride to Cajas. We were grateful, since it would have been dangerous for Fr. Angelus to walk the ten miles up the mountain. Thus, the day began for us, without coffee and without food. We learned how difficult it is not to have anything to drink. Food, we could manage without. But, having nothing to drink throughout the day was a new experience for us.

We spent most of the day in the Garden. Prayers were being led over a portable sound system, and the general attitude was one of reverence and patient waiting for the announcement of the time of the Virgin's arrival. The priests were kept busy blessing religious articles which the young people would receive from the people who were around the outside of the fence of the Garden and bring to one of the priests in the Garden. Confessions were also being heard throughout the area.

The rain continued, and walking became difficult, as the number of persons moving around had turned the soil into a black, slippery mud. It also became more difficult to cross over the little mountain streams, and there were several of them, which seemed to become more rapid and wider as the rain continued.

The Rose

I was impressed with the people's simple manifestation of love for Our Lady as they brought beautiful bouquets of flowers to adorn the garden area and to be put before her statue near the big rock. Each time another beautiful bouquet of roses was brought in, usually by the young people who walked on their knees up the garden path to the statue, I thought how much I wanted to take a rose home with me. The desire for a rose had welled up within me earlier in the day when I first saw the Garden decked with so many beautiful flowers, most of them roses of every color imaginable.

But, each time I had that thought, I also had the thought that I could not "steal" one of Mary's roses. First, the flowers were given to her, and second, I would be giving bad example by walking out of the Garden with a rose in my hand; and, I didn't have anything with which to snip one off in order to conceal it in my pocket or purse. So, each time I would have the desire for a rose, I would also dialogue with myself why I couldn't have one.

Around three o'clock we received word that Patricia was coming to the Garden, because Our Lady had told her she would appear soon. I positioned myself along the path, kneeling down behind a large basket of long stemmed, red roses. Once again, I dialogued with myself about a rose. Since it had been raining most of the day, I looked for a spot that wasn't muddy where I could put my purse and tote bag. The ground under the bouquet had been somewhat protected and I tucked them under the flowers. Following the apparition, I began to gather up my things to leave and, as I lifted up my purse, I saw a beautiful red rose on the ground next to it. Picking up the rose, I carefully examined it and realized that it had not been broken off, but it was a freshly cut, red rose. Deep in my heart, I knew that it was Our Lady's gift to me. I clutched it in my hand and tenderly kissed it, saying my "thank you" over and over again to Mary. I was deeply moved by her compassionate love for me and my simple desire for a rose. Then, slowly, I wrapped it in a tissue and put it into my pocket, still conscious of not giving bad example by walking out of the Garden with one of Mary's roses. I still have it. Each time I look at it, I experience once again Mary's tender love, who cares so much for each of us that she even responds to the simplest desires of our hearts.

The Apparition

Having been present with the visionaries in Medugorje many times during the reported apparitions, I was careful to watch Patricia during her reported visit from Our Lady. I experienced the same kind of inner peace and sense of a heavenly presence as when I was in Medugorje. There was something deep inside me that convinced me that Our Lady was there. It is impossible for me to explain the sensation because it is more of the heart than of feelings. Patricia responded in a manner quite similar to the visionaries in Medugorje, looking intently up at a single spot, and being completely unaware of anyone or anything around her. I gazed at the spot, too, but didn't see anything supernatural. I didn't need to; I believed the Virgin was there.

Shortly before Patricia had entered the Garden, the rain had changed from a soft, gentle rain, to a hard downpour. It continued throughout the time of apparition and afterwards. Patricia didn't seem to be bothered by the rain. She prayed, went into ecstasy, and spoke the message. Later, after she left the Garden, the message was read over the sound system for everyone to hear. Parts of the message were quoted in an earlier chapter, but the entire message bears repetition here.

> Little children, do not be anguished. Sow happiness and give joy to the world. My little children, I love you much. I am happy with what you have offered on this day. Jesus is present here and in each one of your hearts that has been purified today. We have begun the hard times. They will be ten very sad years. Time is short.
>
> I am expecting you the first Saturday of March and my physical presence among you will conclude then. But I will always remain here to pour out my blessings. Atheism and materialism are eating the world. My priests, religious, laity, work in the work of my Son, Jesus, and convert souls. In the hands of priests and religious is the salvation of souls. Evangelize with the light of my Son, Jesus.
>
> Have pity on my Son in order that my Son will have pity on you before the Father.
>
> I bless you in the name of the Father, in the name of the Son, and in the name of the Spirit of God. Amen

We were told that the Holy Mother had requested that we remain on the mountain until 6:00 that evening, the time for the Angelus prayer. And so, we did. The next day, we interviewed Patricia again, and she described her experience of the day before. She also told us that the Holy Virgin had given the three of us a ''special blessing, because through you the truth would be made known to the world.'' We didn't fully understand the meaning of that, and we remain in a posture of expectation, waiting for the proper way to carry it out.

March 3, 1990

Having heard in the message that March would be the last visit of Mary to Patricia, I sensed that I would be returning for it. How, I didn't know, but that I would be there, I did know. Fr. Augustine Donegan accompanied me in March. Once again, we spent the night in vigil on the mountain. It was even colder and more rainy than in February. Even though we had access to a tent close by the Garden, it was a difficult night. Daylight didn't bring much relief. Over one hundred thousand persons spent the night on the mountain, and even more came as daylight broke. The atmosphere, once again, was one of prayerful expectation. Mary came at twelve-twenty in the afternoon, rather than at three-forty as she had in February. Her message brought tears to people's eyes, as they heard her express her love for us and her sorrow at having to leave us.

Fr. Augustine and I were present in the Garden, near Patricia, for the apparition. Members of the Bishop's second Commission were also there, along with the media. It was the first time that professional television cameras or the press had been permitted in the Garden. That evening and for the next two days, television news reports were full of the events at El Cajas. The message from Our Lady was broadcast over and over again throughout the country, and into neighboring countries and the events made the front page of many of the newspapers in the country.

The Last Apparition

Patricia's experience of Our Lady was intense, and she knelt with her body arched backwards, her head tilted so far back that I wondered how she could stay in that position for any length of time. I watched her as she looked toward the sky, and began conversing silently. Then, she began to speak aloud in a pitch slightly higher than her normal voice. The tone was delicate and sweet, and pleasing to listen to. She spoke in the first person. This phenomenon was not new. Many times Our Lady gave her messages to the people in this manner. This was the message that caused many people to cry:

> My little children, small of heart, today I have brought you here so that you may love the Heart of my Son, Jesus. Little children, I love you very much. Today is the day of my physical retreat, but my spiritual retreat will never be. I will be with you always, little children. I ask for prayer, fasting, penance. Help those in most need. Children, in the end God will triumph over all things. Remember the first commandment of my Son, Jesus: Love one another, and love God above all things. Little children, I ask for peace, pardon, and conversion.
>
> Children, priests and religious, help in the conversion of the world, the redemption of souls, the purification. Children, the laity, help in the conversion. Young people, be examples of light. Carry the Cross in your hearts. Put on humility. Children, white doves of peace, be the light. The sick are indeed chosen by God, chosen for the redemption of the world. Little children, I love you so much that even for me it gives me sorrow to say goodbye to you. Children, I am not going to leave you ever, because I will be here and I will wait for you always, just as (I have) each month, each time that you came here to leave your sadnesses, your sorrows, your anguishes. Little children, each representative of each country, I ask you to take the message of peace, love and understanding.
>
> Children, I give you the blessing of the all-powerful God, Father, Son and Holy Spirit. Come always to visit me. Never abandon me, little ones, because I love you so much, so much. At the end of all the apparitions in the world, I will leave a great sign in this place and in all those where I have been. Goodbye my little ones. Goodbye my children.

After the message, Patricia leaned over to the ground, almost as if to kiss it. She remained bent over for a short time and then straightening up to a normal kneeling posture, looked up again and began to sing the *Ave Maria* aloud. Smiling at the end of it, she bowed her head, and then rose to her feet. The apparition was over, and so were her visits from the beautiful Lady. There was a silence in the Garden, as people pondered the message, and realized that our heavenly Mother's visitations to Patricia were over. Patricia told us that Our Lady would be there always, to hear our prayers and to pray for us. She also said that the Holy Mother wanted her children to come in procession every First Saturday, beginning at 5:00 in the morning and staying until the Noon Angelus when she would bless everyone.

We left the mountain shortly after that. There was sadness and, at the same time, joy. We had experienced the love of our heavenly Mother who was leaving us physically, but who would always be with us spiritually.

The next day we visited with Patricia and asked her to talk about her experience of the day before. She was surprisingly happy and peaceful. She told us that as twelve o'clock came closer, she began to feel anxiety, because she knew that it would be the last visit from Our Lady. As she described the apparition she smiled softly, recalling the events of the day before.

During the time of apparition, Patricia spoke the message Our Lady was giving to all of her children. I asked Patricia if she was aware that she was speaking the message. She shook her head, saying "No," and continued to relate what she remembered from the experience. The last apparition was the most beautiful she had had. but as the time came for Mary to leave, Patricia knew that Mary was sad because she "had to say goodbye to us." And so, Patricia decided to sing the *Ave Maria* because "it pleases Mary when we pray the Hail Mary." After she finished singing, the apparition ended. Mary continued to speak to her in her heart, but Patricia did not see her anymore.

For me, the experience was very deep. For some reason I had been drawn into the events with Patricia. Even though

I spoke only a little Spanish, and Patricia spoke only a little English, we were able to communicate. Most of the time, however, we had an interpreter with us. After I returned home, I realized that the experiences of February and March had begun to take deep root within me, and I began to sense the call to write this book. Mary's messages were so important, and most timely, and they needed to get out to all people.

Rome, Medugorje, and Assisi

It was only a matter of weeks after we returned from Ecuador, when I received word that Patricia was going to Rome to present our Holy Father with a message from Our Lady, and that she wanted to go on to Medugorje for a personal visit there. Since I have been to Medugorje many times, I was asked what was the best way for her to go there from Rome. Deep within me, I knew that I should be with her and immediately I began to make arrangements to meet them in Rome.

Msgr. Vincent Thu, one of the Papal Secretaries, had arranged for Patricia, her mother and Bernardita to be seated in the front row of the audience hall, where Our Holy Father would greet them. Patricia and Bernardita had prepared a lengthy document that was given to Our Holy Father several days earlier. On the day of the audience, April 4, 1990, Patricia carried with her a small envelope that contained the hand written, personal message from Our Lady for the Holy Father. Having been told to identify themselves as being from Ecuador, Patricia, her mother and Bernardita were greeted by Our Holy Father and received his blessing. Patricia handed him the personal letter she had written. He accepted it saying, ''We are together.''

Patricia's friends who had come from Ecuador and I were in another section of the audience hall, but we were able to see Our Holy Father greeting them. The official Papal photographer captured the meeting on film, prints of which we were able to obtain later.

Two days later, we flew to Medugorje. During our visit there, Patricia relived her visitations from Mary when she met Marija and Ivan. She said she felt as if she already knew them because Our Lady had told her about them in response to a question Patricia had asked our Lady. The visionaries shared what their lives were like before the apparitions, and how they have changed. Patricia spoke a word of advice to each of them, telling them that they should begin now to prepare spiritually for the day when Our Lady's visits would end. She told them that Satan becomes real in the days after Our Lady's visitations cease, and they need to be preparing now for that day.

I returned to Ecuador for the month of October, 1990, in order to gather the material for this book and for a second book, a documentary, now in preparation, but which will take some time to complete, since I want it to be as accurate as possible with dates, documents, reports and the testimonies of witnesses.

My red rose, in its glass container, is a constant reminder of our Mother's gentle love for me. In drawing me closer to herself, she has also drawn me closer to the Merciful Heart of her Son, Jesus. My consecration to Jesus through her has taken on deeper meaning and each day is a new venture in the path of life, which I do not walk alone, but in the constant company of Mary, who is not only my Mother, but my guide, my model, my friend, and my sister.

God's Plan

There is always a reason for everything. Sometimes we know what it is, and at other times, we are left to wonder. God had a reason why I should be invited to go to Ecuador, and God had a reason why Fr. Michael and Fr. Angelus should accompany me in February, and a reason why Fr. Augustine should go with me in March. While each of us had a different experience, we all had the same experience. This book would be incomplete without their testimonies. And so, I have asked each of the priests to share his experiences in Ecuador.

Fr. Michael Scanlan, T.O.R.

The call to go to Cuenca seemed clear to me. It was a natural extension of our pilgrimage to Guadalupe and a supernatural grace urging us to go to Cuenca to experience the Guadalupe Apparition of today. Indeed, in Mexico, I was greatly impacted by the centrality of Mary the Mother of God being our mother. This truth overshadowed all other aspects of the Guadalupe apparitions and miracles.

The morning of February 1, 1990, we left Mexico City for Quito, Ecuador. I was experiencing a rather violent attack of that intestinal virus called "Montezuma's Revenge." This incapacitated me so that Fr. Angelus and Sr. Isabel had to help me to walk, and when we arrived in Quito, I went directly to bed.

The next day we traveled to Cuenca where the doctor told me I could go to El Cajas provided I was driven to the 11,000 foot location. I experienced strong movements of grace to enable me to walk the ten miles up the mountain and then to pray for three hours the next morning in the Garden. At 2:00 in the afternoon, as we waited for Patricia to come for the apparition, I suddenly saw the Garden area enveloped in light. I heard the singing and the praying of the people increase in volume and fervor. It seemed as if we were caught up in a supernatural aura. My heart beat quickly with expectation and then I sensed strongly within me Our Lady speaking the following words:

> "Michael, receive and accept me deep in your heart as your mother. That is what I am and wish to be. You do not turn to me in life's circumstances; for I would nurture you, free you and protect you while I lead you on the path of the cross of my Son. Receive now, open up to me now. Let me fill you and bless you. Seek me, your mother and you will never be alone."

I stood transfixed for sometime; then as I recovered, I knelt in thanksgiving. As I looked around, the singing and praying seemed muted and the weather was gloomy and semi-dark. I left the Garden and inquired of two men about my experience of the glowing light, but neither of them had noticed it happening.

I had a certainty within me that the apparition would happen at 3:00 P.M., the hour of Christ's death. I mentioned this to some companions and then I reentered the Garden to wait. I experienced Our Lady leading me and preparing me. When Patricia came into the Garden, walking on her knees, it seemed to me that this was normal and right for the occasion. As she led us in prayer, I knew Our Lady would appear to her. I wondered whether I would see her. When Patricia went into ecstasy, I looked very briefly at her and then focused my gaze at where Patricia was seeing her. I simply believed and prayed prayers of thanksgiving. I did not see anything supernatural, though my spirit was held by a supernatural grace of faith, hope and love. As Patricia began to leave, I joined in giving the priestly blessing and praying for people who asked for prayer.

Then, I heard the message in English. One set of words pierced into my heart and grasped my mind as true, "We have begun the hard times. They will be ten very sad years. Time is short." I was settled in my mind that the Lord had sent his Mother to prepare us for the these times and help us through them.

The next day, when we visited Patricia, I related my experience. She affirmed that what I heard Our Lady say is the message she (Our Lady) wants each person to receive. She also spoke to us about the hard times and we discussed how long that might be. She thought from some earlier messages that they might be six years in length. The time Our Lady had indicated was in fact remaining before the year 2000.

Patricia showed us the pictures with oil on them and the Sacred Host given her by St. Michael, the Archangel. I was curious, but somewhat doubtful, as I came closer to view the Host. I saw clearly a depiction of the Madonna and Child on the Host. Our Lady was holding up Jesus and presenting him to us. It was a beautiful picture, very artistic in flowing congruent lines. Jesus was reaching out with his hands towards me. I knew the Host was truly the Body of Christ. I gazed at the picture until Patricia moved to return it to its encasing. I had certainty in my heart that God had given me this sign so I would believe. I can, to this day, in a moment, reflect and see the picture again.

I spoke with Patricia about this and she then told us the Our Lady had given a special blessing to the three of us so that we could convey her message to the world. I wasn't sure what that meant, though I knew I would testify to the truth of all that I had seen. Fr. Angelus and I then celebrated a wonderful Mass of thanksgiving with Patricia and her family participating, in the room next to the altar of the Host.

The effect of my experience in Cuenca has been a deepening of my devotion to Our Lady as well as a deepening of my entrustment and consecration to Jesus through Mary. I have a renewed appreciation for other Marian apparitions and a strengthened appreciation of the urgency of our times. I pray the Rosary and the Chaplet of Divine Mercy at least daily. I know the graces which I have received are to be shared and I look for God's leading as to how and when to do so.

Fr. Angelus Migliore, T.O.R.

In the fall of 1989, when I heard about a proposed pilgrimage to the shrine of Our Lady of Guadalupe in Mexico City, I had a spiritual sense that I should ask permission to accompany the pilgrimage as a chaplain. I had always had a strong devotion to the Blessed Mother, and while I knew very little about Guadalupe, I was attracted to this apparition. Later, when I found out that Sr. Isabel and Fr. Michael were planning to go from Guadalupe to Ecuador, I had the same spiritual urging that I should also ask to accompany them.

Because it worked out so easily for me to go on both trips, I felt that I was truly responding to a grace to participate in events that would change me forever.

At Guadalupe, I was brought into a deeper spiritual relationship with the Blessed Virgin Mary, particularly as Mother and as Protectress. I came to experience her as a guard and guardian of my life and my vocation in a deeper way than I had before. Today, I understand that this grace, which I see as the foundational grace of the apparitions in Ecuador, was important for me to appreciate and to understand what was happening in Cuenca, Ecuador.

Our arrival in Quito, Ecuador was significantly dramatic because of Fr. Michael's illness. I am sure that Satan tried to use Fr. Michael's sickness to try to sideline him, because his experience and insights were essential for us to make an appropriate evaluation of the events. Satan lost, because with medical help, Fr. Michael continued to improve and he was in good condition when his expertise was needed.

We were met at the airport in Cuenca by the wife of Gaston Ramirez and Bernardita Jerves de Ugalde, the principal companion of Patricia, the visionary. I rode to Patricia's home with Bernardita who began to tell me the story of the apparitions, about which I knew very little.

Our meeting with Pachi deeply moved me. Because I understood Spanish fairly well I was able to participate in the interview directly. I found Pachi a lovely, young woman who had evidently experienced God very deeply. Her presence exhibited peace even amidst the certain confusion of our arrival. She knew we were there to interview her and to make an evaluation of the authenticity of her experiences. Yet, she treated us with simple respect, willing to answer our questions, but without trying to prove anything. She was totally without guile, very normal and joyful. Our entire interview was very relaxed and well interspersed with humor and laughing.

I found Patricia to be a girl of average intelligence and limited experience in matters of Church teaching and Marian Apparitions. Yet, when Fr. Michael presented her with questions that demanded nuanced responses, she was perfect in her answers. I knew immediately that something profound was happening to her, beyond normal explanations. Her responses went beyond her natural intelligence or experience. Even if an expert had drilled correct answers into her, the way she responded and the depth of her understanding were far beyond the normal maturation of a seventeen years old high school student with average intelligence.

Because my experience of Patricia, and also of Bernardita, convinced me that something profound was happening in their lives, I then turned my attention to determine if I could uncover any influence of evil in the whole matter. I have had some experience in the area of evil, and I have a certain competence in discerning the work of the devil. By the time I left Cuenca, I was convinced that the events in Cuenca and the experience of Patricia, Bernardita, and others are of divine origin.

After Mass Friday evening, we began to climb the mountain to El Cajas. (I fully intend to ask the Blessed Virgin when I meet her why she has such a fascination for mountains and rocky places.) The climb was dramatic for me, because I did it on the back of a motorcycle, arriving at the Garden around eleven o'clock. I was separated from Fr. Michael and Sr. Isabel, but because of my Spanish, I did well enough. I spent the entire night in the Garden and I spent it in a prayer vigil. It was cold and rainy, yet I did not experience abnormal fatigue. I have a serious heart condition and the combination of high altitude, inclement weather and natural fatigue, in primitive conditions, should had affected me adversely. Naturally, I was concerned, but I moved with a spiritual sense that I was doing what God wanted of me and he was protecting my health.

About nine o'clock in the morning, I caught up with Fr. Michael and Sr. Isabel. During the day, I stayed in the Garden most of the time, praying and hearing confessions. I heard confessions of upper class Spanish Ecuadorians as well as of Ecuadorian Indians. They were all filled with great faith and, I recognized that the apparition events were effecting deep conversion in their lives.

Around three o'clock in the afternoon, I sensed the Blessed Virgin Mary's presence, even though Pachi and Bernardita had not yet arrived. They came shortly after three. It was a thrilling experience for me to participate in the apparition. I knelt about ten feet away from Pachi and I heard her as the message from Our Lady was spoken. I understood almost all that was said and noted that the voice was much different from Patricia's normal voice. It seemed much higher pitched to me. During the entire time that Patricia was in ecstasy, I had the same sense of Mary's presence that I had when I was privileged to participate in a reported apparition in Medugorje. I don't think there are words to express the feeling I had when I heard the words that came from Pachi's lips, and the emotion in them, as the Virgin said, "Have mercy on my Son so that my Son will have mercy on you before the Father.'' To this day, those searing words continue to burn in my heart and bring me to the reality of the pain of sin and the cost of my sin to my most loving Savior and to his Blessed Mother.

Later, when we learned that Mary had also looked on the three of us and gave us a special blessing, I was very humbled. The Blessed Virgin said that we would make her message known throughout the world. I am grateful that this book is part of doing that.

The next day when we visited with Patricia and her family, we continued to see more signs of God's special favor in demonstrating the veracity of the apparitions. There were the holy cards that sweated oil and the miraculous, Sacred Host. But, while I was moved by these, it was the faith of the people and the many, many conversions to God that convinced me of the authenticity of the apparitions to Patricia.

The Blessed Virgin herself, tied her message to Patricia to that of Guadalupe and revealed herself as a Mother who will protect her children by teaching them the truth. For me, that is the central reality and that is why the grace of Guadalupe was a necessary first step for me. Our Lady chose Guadalupe as the place to commission Patricia to tell everyone about her messages. This, I believe, was intentional, so that we, in the Americas, could know her special motherly love and care for us.

Without any doubt, this experience for me was life changing. To be present at such a great event is a special grace. I know that I have experienced a deeper, personal conversion. The mercy of God is so personal that I experience it now as I never have before. I look upon Mary as my Mother who has invited me to share her life and who has opened for me the same path that she chose to take to the Father. Her messages are personal encouragements for me to live the graces that are being poured out in these days. I now know how deeply my personal sin touches Jesus and pains him. I understand the urgency to come to Him daily and to receive him, with greater devotion, in the Eucharist. I delight to be in His presence and I beg Mary to keep me there always.

The messages from the Blessed Mother to Patricia speak especially to our hemisphere and to the dangers that we face from the enemy. In these days when sin is so flagrant and blasphemy is evidenced not only in words, but in people's life style, God is showing us His mercy by affirming the truth of his love. His Mother is sent to us to point us to the way of receiving that love. She cautions us that continued sin and selfishness have their consequences, and in every age mankind has had to pay for his rebellion against God. Therefore, conversion to the mercy of Jesus is necessary in these days of our age, perhaps more necessary than before, because sin continues to grow in men's hearts. As men's hearts continue to become colder, we must pray for the fire of Divine Love to be enkindled again in our day. I pray that as you read the words of this book, the love of Jesus may fill your heart, as it has mine.

Fr. Augustine Donegan, T.O.R.

It was at dinner on Sunday evening, February 26, 1990, that Fr. Michael Scanlan suggested that I accompany Sr. Isabel to Ecuador to be present for the last alleged apparition of the Blessed Mother to Patricia Talbott. It was not that I did not love Our Lady, but Ecuador was so far away. It was really in another country and I knew that the Blessed Mother was very much here in Steubenville. Sr. Isabel was a bit hesitant that I should go. Because of the strenuous experience she had had the month before, she was concerned about my physical health. The mountain was cold and rainy and she knew that I had been suffering with arthritis pain in my knees. But, after praying, I told Fr. Michael Scanlan that I was "ready and willing." Sr. Isabel agreed. And, believe me, never have I regretted that decision.

And so, at 8:00 on Thursday morning, March 1, 1990, we boarded a plane in Pittsburgh and, at 7:30 that evening, found ourselves in Quito, Ecuador. Our hostess, Irene, was at the airport waiting for us. The hospitality of her home made the long trip worthwhile in every way.

On the following morning, the three of us flew to Cuenca, Ecuador, the home town of Patricia Talbott, the visionary.

After celebrating Eucharist and enjoying some lunch, we made our way to Patricia's home to keep our appointment with her. When we entered her home, we sensed a reverential stillness and peace. We quickly learned that the pictures on the little altar in Patricia's room were weeping, and we were invited to go upstairs to see them. I can not explain my feelings at that moment. It was the first time I had seen the phenomenon that has been reported as happening in other holy places. We knelt and prayed for awhile in the room, and then began our visit with Patricia.

What impressed me the most about Patricia was her beautiful sincerity and utter simplicity. Irene was our interpreter and it was a most pleasant visit. The questions we asked were very simply answered and somehow, we knew we were standing "on holy ground."

As we were leaving Patricia to prepare to go to the site of the apparition for an all night vigil, half-jokingly, I said to Patricia, "When you see Our Lady tomorrow, say 'hello' for us." And she lovingly responded, "I will." With this we left and began our trip "up the mountain."

Fortunately, we were able to drive to El Cajas, the site of the apparitions. I was overwhelmed by what I first experienced. Literally, there were thousands of people all over the hillsides, praying. And that continued throughout the night, even though it was bitter cold and it rained most of the night. There were many who did not even have the protection of a tent. We were fortunate in having one.

The next morning at 7:30 I found myself in "Our Lady's Garden," the place where the Lady is said to appear,—waiting, with well over 100,000 people. I had spent part of the night sitting outside our tent, and the rest lying on the ground inside the tent trying to get some sleep. What time on Saturday the apparition would take place—even Patricia was awaiting the word. So, I stood most of the next five hours near the statue of Mary in the Garden, praying and being caught up in wonder at the number of persons who had weathered the night and who, like me, were prayerfully waiting for Our Lady to come. The rain continued throughout the entire day, and it was very cold.

It was just about Noon that Patricia entered "Our Lady's Garden." This was the signal for which all these people were waiting. It sounded to me like the rustling of leaves as everyone knelt. The moment was awesome as I watched Patricia intently. She knelt and began to pray—just as you or I would begin to pray. Within a moment I could see that she was caught up in an ecstatic state. I know that in this mystical state all the natural senses lose contact with their surroundings. I recalled that in the case of Bernadette of Lourdes in the year 1878, that during the time she was in ecstasy, she did not even feel a burning candle under her arm. And now, I could hear a beautiful voice speaking through Patricia, "I have brought you here so that you may love the heart of my Son, Jesus." Patricia herself did not even hear the voice. The Spanish was clear and beautiful.

The extraordinary phenomenon that happened here was that the words coming out of the Visionary did not match the movement of her lips. As Patricia was talking with Our Lady, Our Lady was talking to us. It was an overwhelmingly beautiful experience. Two days later when we returned to Quito, the Morning Television News was still carrying the event and we watched and heard everything again. It was truly spectacular—to say the least.

That Saturday afternoon, as we prepared to leave the Garden site, I realized that I had never thought about using the knee brace that I had carried with me all the way from Steubenville. The arthritis in my knees never bothered me at all! This was most unusual. Normally, the slightest change in the weather causes me pain. I knew that Our Lady had strengthened me for that time I was in her garden in El Cajas. Sr. Isabel's fears never materialized, and we both rejoiced and thanked Our Lady for her care for me.

Sunday morning, we were back with Patricia in her home in Cuenca. She told us that the day before, Jesus, under the Sign of Mercy, accompanied Our Lady. Also, there were seven angels present and another person whom all of us at Steubenville love very much—the one we call our holy Father. His name is Francis—and he came from a little town in Italy called Assisi. When I reminded Patricia that Frs. Michael,

Angelus and I were all Franciscans, and that we had come from Franciscan University, she said, ''Maybe that is a sign for you.''

Just before we left to begin a seven hour automobile trip to Quito, (the plane was not operating due to mechanical problems), I said to Patricia—and at the time I was really joking because of the spectacular experience of Saturday, but still I asked,—''Pachi, did you say 'hello' to Our Lady for us?'' Her face actually lit up and she responded, ''Father, I forgot to tell you that I did, and when I told her, she smiled and said, 'I love and protect all my children.' ''

As a final parting gift, Patricia took us to her bedroom where she removed a little golden pyx from a wooden box and handed it to me. ''Open it, and look inside,'' she said. I fell to my knees as I beheld the Eucharistic host and listened to the story of its miraculous appearance on her altar. She told us that later that day, Fr. Teran would celebrate Mass there for her family and the little host would be broken and consumed by herself and those present. I told her that when I walked into her room the first time, I almost genuflected as one does in reverence to the Blessed Sacrament in a church. Little did I know then that Jesus was truly present on her altar in Eucharistic form. Truly, all of us there believed we were standing ''on holy ground.''

EPILOGUE

THE GARDEN IN EL CAJAS

During the time Patricia was in Rome and Medugorje, the statue of Mary, Guardian of the Faith, and the statue of the Sacred Heart in the Garden at El Cajas were vandalized. They were thrown to the ground and the head and hands were broken off of the statues. The cross was broken and the arch in front of the rock, requested by the Virgin, was pulled down. The ownership of the land within the Garden and immediately surrounding it is in dispute. The followers of the reported apparitions have purchased a section of it, but a small segment remains disputed by a neighbor.

The statues have been repaired; the cross and the arch repositioned, just like the Holy Virgin had requested originally. The Sacred Heart statue has been put back on top of the rock, and the statue of the Guardian of the Faith now occupies its position in front of and to the left of the rock. An Indian family lives in the ''tool shed'' which has been fixed up to make a nice home and they provide protection in the area as much as is possible.

Many people frequent El Cajas, finding there quiet and peace. On any given day, if you went there, you would probably find that you were not alone. The First Saturdays continue to be the days on which pilgrims visit ''Our Lady'' at the Garden in El Cajas.

The movement of the ''Guardian of the Faith'' has been established to promote the living of the messages, and to organize the monthly First Saturday pilgrimages that the Virgin requested. This organization has been approved by the

Bishops of Ibarra and Guayaquil. The Bishop of Quito has approved the organization in principle, but is concerned about the title "Guardian of the Faith." However, in May, 1991, a public chapel, located in a section of Quito, was dedicated to Mary under the title "Guardian of the Faith." The Bishop of Cuenca has not recognized the group to date.

Patricia

Patricia graduated from high school in July, 1990. In the days since the last apparition, she has experienced loneliness and depression. Living without the consolation of her heavenly Mother's regular visits is difficult for her. Nevertheless, she knew she had to move on with her life and her mission, for the Holy Mother had told her "you know what you have to do."

Patricia sought spiritual direction and assistance in discerning the next step in her life. Her desire to be married came into focus, and her spiritual director, with the assistance of a Jesuit priest at the Jesuit College in Cuenca, helped her discern that step. The Holy Virgin had left her free to choose her state in life. Patricia believed that she would be able to carry out her mission as a married woman, especially since her fiance supported her in that call. Together they made the Spiritual Exercises of St. Ignatius and discerned their call to marriage.

On January 19, 1991, Patricia and Andres Vega Cordova were united in the Sacrament of Matrimony. The Archbishop had originally agreed to officiate at the ceremony, but at the last minute was unable to do so. Fr. Julio Teran celebrated the wedding Mass and received their vows. At midnight, following a private reception, Patricia and Andres, still in their wedding attire, went to El Cajas to present themselves to the Holy Virgin and to leave Patricia's bridal bouquet there as a token of their love and devotion to her.

Patricia and Andres have committed themselves to carrying out the Virgin's wishes to serve the beggars, the sick and the lepers. They participate in a weekly support group for married persons who are seeking to live the Holy Virgin's messages and to grow deeper in their Catholic faith. Patricia has established a group who visit a local clinic regularly. She assists in "little ways" with serving the poor, such as training poor children to receive their First Holy Communion.

The Holy Virgin told Patricia she would speak to her in her heart when there was a special need or difficult moment. On February 22, 1991 Patricia experienced a locution for the first time since the last apparition in March, 1990. Patricia was having a difficult day. She was sad and "low in faith." Alone in her bedroom, she started to cry. She heard the words, "My dear child," twice. At first, she thought it was her imagination, but then she began to smell flowers, and heard "My dear child" again. She realized that it was the Holy Virgin and went to the little altar she had made at the end of a small hall. She clearly heard the Virgin speaking to her. When the Virgin stopped speaking, Patricia wrote what she had heard. The Virgin spoke to her about her own role in coming to people all over the world, and of the necessity, not only for ourselves but for others, for us to hear her messages and respond to them with faithful conversion. The message is tender and reveals a loving Mother who is concerned about all her children.

> Listen, my children. Blessed be you in the name of the Lord.
>
> My Son Jesus had John the Baptist as a precursor for His first coming, when He came as Redeemer. Now, my children, He has me, His Mother, as precursor for when He will come as judge.
>
> Change soon, soon, little children, or I, myself, will continue crying tears for all eternity.
>
> Children, because I call you softly, you do not answer my calls. My Son will stand firmly with me because He knows I am His Mother and He knows how much I love you. Is this how you ignore my love, my loved ones? Do not be irresponsible or ungrateful for the graces you have received, and do not destroy the bridges that I have laid for you.

Do not fear for yourselves, since you do listen to Me. But there are many who do not listen and they need you, children. And, if you have stopped listening to me, return to me again so you will not be stupid and condemn yourself.

Every time you go farther and farther away, my dear children, think clearly to determine what comes from God and what from the devil. Be careful about false prophets who will confuse you and who will win your attention with beautiful words.

My Children, I am a woman, but I have firm hands. I, myself, will sign the Cross of Christ on you, I, the precursor of all the works of my Son.

Man lives pressed by time and for the world. My Son gave you time in which to adore Him and bless Him, but you do not give Him your prayers nor offer Him your hearts; you just ignore Him. Man is by and for man, and not by and for God.

Now I want to leave with you these words that I left for you at Cana of Galilee, "Do whatever He tells you."

And I make a call for prayer, for fasting, for penance. And I promise to all those children who will pray the Rosary with great devotion that, in the fifth mystery, the Archangels Michael, Rafael, and Gabriel will sign the Cross on your foreheads.

Your Mother, the Guardian of the Faith.

Our Mother's messages are serious. We must take them seriously, if we believe that God is sending her to help us to prepare for that day when our stay on this earth is over, and we go to meet our heavenly bridegroom. It is useless for us to fear the "days of darkness" or the "chastisements" if we strive to live each day as the Holy Virgin has asked us, united under her mantle and in the Merciful Heart of her Son, Jesus. She, who is the Guardian of our Faith, has promised to assist us and to lead us to her Son, Jesus, who is our Lord and Savior. And, as our Holy Mother said at the wedding in Cana of Galilee and again to Patricia on February 22, 1991, "Do whatever He tells you to do."